CORRIDORS IN THE SKY

Dearest Mike & Mikaela,

Here's proof there is no "manger" too dark or smelly for Christ to appear & change everything for the better! May your darkest night produce the Light of the world.

Sincerely,

Robert S. Totman

CORRIDORS
IN THE SKY

REVELATIONS OF A NEW YORK 9/11 AIR TRAFFIC CONTROLLER

ROBERT S. TOTMAN

Published by RSTvictory.com, ND
Library of Congress Control Number:
2016916279

print ISBN: 978-0-9979528-1-0
ebook ISBN: 978-0-9979528-0-3

Produced by Retelling
www.Retelling.net

in association with Samizdat Creative
www.samizdatcreative.com

Cover design by Cynthia Young
www.youngdesign.biz

Cover images: © Peeter Viisimaa / iStock, © Chris Downie / iStock,
© Todd Quackenbush

CONTENTS

This book is dedicated to Truth, which is not subject to the will of people and does not change, for their own benefit.

FOREWORD

In 2010, my marriage was struggling, my husband was deep in depression and in a desperate attempt to find anyone who could help, he "happened upon" Robert and Susan Totman during an internet search, and he sent Robert a few questions.

We were driving down the interstate as my husband read Robert's reply out loud. It was the first moment of hope I'd felt in a long time. It was as if God breathed life in and through us, and I couldn't believe it was coming from total strangers hundreds of miles away–in exactly the right way, at the right time.

The Totmans have fascinated me since this beginning. Here is a couple with four children who literally gave away all they possessed in order to live their lives in abandon for God. They don't ask for anything; they literally live and die on the breath of God. And that draws me to them. They are the real deal.

The story ahead is why they are the real deal. You will see what they have endured: the highs of a financially successful air traffic controller, an affair, brokenness, and addiction. But ultimately this is the story of how our all-powerful God redeemed the lives of Robert and Susan Totman out of the ashes and rubble of 9/11.

I am changed because of Christ's work through them. I am so thankful to have met them and believe the story that lies ahead will touch and move you deeply. To God be the glory for He makes a way in the desert and streams in the wasteland (Is. 43:19)!

Kristin Sukraw
President at Reliant Studios and Nonprofit Film School

LIFE'S A BEACH

I was chasing something but never finding it. At first I thought it was the thrill of the wave. Out of the waters of the Atlantic Ocean along the Jacksonville Beaches near my home sometimes rose glassy, perfectly formed, shoulder to head high waves perfect for thrilling rides that paralleled the long, broad, sandy beaches.

As a teenager I would get out of bed in the morning, eat breakfast, grab my board and walk to the beach to surf. All. Day. Long. It was calming and soothing and exciting all at the same time to sit out in the water for hours, watching the sets come in and gauging exactly which wave in a set was the one sent just for me. I was willing to pay whatever price was necessary to be one with their beauty, power, and form. Sometimes I'd wait a whole day or many days without partaking in a single satisfying thrill. I didn't want to spend my energy trying to catch anything less than the very best.

When I identified a choice wave, I kicked into action, paddling with all my might in order to join with it, allowing it to lift me up into its own course so that I could flow with it and find its nuances of perfection. While racing with the wind in my face, I celebrated the final leg of its long journey home to the shore. I got to be its welcome-home committee. In my mind the wave rejoiced with fulfillment, because it had come so far to use its last bit of strength to give me delight. My joy proved its journey was not in vain. I would say to myself, *That was awesome! Quick, let me get right back out there before I miss the next celebration!*

Chasing the wave was an all-consuming passion for a young season of my life. I didn't think much about having friends or going out or getting a job or an education or, really, anything else. I just wanted to get out there, into the water, where my peace and joy were waiting. There I would remain for up to twelve hours a day. I wouldn't even get out of the water to eat, because those precious waves meant even more to me than food. Oh, but after twelve hours of surfing, you can rest assured that when I got home I raided our refrigerator. As I laid my head on my pillow at night the waves continued; I was among them, going to sweet sleep with my love. I would wake the next morning and do it all over again.

I didn't care too much for school. I was bored with it. It just didn't seem to have anything to offer me compared to the ocean that was a mere few blocks away from where I went to high school. There were many days that my love for the water outweighed attending high school, and I regularly maxed out the number of allowed absences. I think I graduated on the graces of my Home Economics teacher, that one last required elective. I didn't deserve to pass Home Economics, an incredibly easy class. We were tasked to bake cookies, balance a checkbook, sew a patch on jeans and the like. This super sweet teacher would roll her eyes at my foolish slothfulness and give me a pass. Without her I would have failed my senior year, not having the required number of electives. She did more for me than she likely realized.

Ah, but the smell of the warm, salty ocean breeze that caressed my sun-soaked, mostly bare hot skin, along with the feeling of the cottony soft sand between my toes, and even the literal taste of the salty water when I first splashed-in, gave me a strong sense that I was home as I paddled out to meet the breaking waves. Nothing could keep me out of the water, away from the curvy motion of those rolling, alluring waves. With the ocean's draw so nearby, it's amazing that I graduated at all.

I was born in Jacksonville, Florida, in 1967, and have an older brother, Ed, and a younger sister, Tina. My father, Ed Sr., was an electrical engineer with Southern Bell, and my mother, Maryann, was a housewife. I loved and appreciated my family very much. It instilled such a strong sense of security, belonging, teamwork and play.

My dad welcomed my brother and me in his aviation-related hobbies, which included building remote control airplanes and model rockets. He also frequently took us to NASA at Cape Canaveral where we marveled at different rocket launches, from the Saturn V to the Space Shuttle and all sorts of in-betweens. For a young child, being at real rocket launches, in person, with the atmosphere rumbling throughout my entire little body shaped my future in ways I couldn't have predicted. The idea of blazing through the sky, farther than I could see, and being taken to outer space made a lasting impact on my impressionable young mind. I thought, *Man can do anything. I can do anything!*

When I was seven years old my father also took me to the Jacksonville Air Route Traffic Control Center (ARTCC, "Jax Center," a radar air traffic control facility), and I'm told that I never stopped talking about it after that day. Actually, I don't even remember that specific visit. But later in life, when I reconnected with my high school friends, they almost all said that I never stopped insisting that one day I'd be an air traffic controller.

It was ironic actually, because I never really liked flying. My brother did. As an adult he has his pilot's license and he hobbies in all sorts of aviation adventures, from skydiving to paragliding and beyond. Our dad provided a culture related to aviation that spurred our interests. I'd have to say these childhood experiences with aviation must have formed me to be a good fit for the industry. It all made so much sense to me. It seemed natural.

One time I out performed my older brother and my father while flying remote control airplanes. I think that was a root to my early aviation passion. It was such a rush because, in my mind, I was a little kid and they were bigger and better than me at everything. Put that remote control in my hands, though, and step back and watch. Yes, it was very natural to me. And the respect it brought me made me feel good—a feeling that I wouldn't have and would be chasing again for quite some time.

When I was in the seventh grade my parents announced their divorce—out of the blue. It was such a shock. I had never even heard them argue. Over the next several years each of my siblings and I had to make impossible decisions.

It felt like a choice between keeping your left arm or your right arm. Which arm would you prefer to have, because you can't have them both. Not only was I the middle child, but now I had my sweet, sweet little nine-year-old sister and precious mother on one side and my cherished big brother and hero father on the other. My father always smelled wonderful when he got home from working amidst the electronics at the phone company. He smelled like my daddy and that distinct, signature aroma pulled me towards him.

There I was, smack in the middle, torn and forced to choose. My little sister and my picture-perfect mother were devastated, and so was I. We seemed to be in the same boat of "I didn't deserve this and it hurts so bad!" My older brother and my father seemed to be in an entirely different boat, some boat of "life goes on and you just have to make the best of it." It felt criminal to have our family in two different boats while there was nothing "our boat" could do about it. It was so sudden and so not the security and belonging and teamwork and play that had become an absolute part of my very own identity. I chose to live with my mother at first, but after a few years of missing my father I moved in with him.

It was tough and I don't recall any sort of coping assistance given to us at all. I don't say that to cast any blame on my parents. It was obvious to me, even at my young age, that as they split up they were each caught up in their own respective dramas. The 1970s in America produced a terrible wave of destruction to my family and so many others through divorce. Seems like somebody said it was just fine to throw a grenade into family units, and so very many adults took the notion hook, line, and sinker. Looking back, I'm amazed that I didn't pick up any terrible habits to cope with the shock and pain (or maybe they surfaced later in life, as I'll share in subsequent chapters). Just tears on my pillow, that's all. Lots of tears, alone, night after night. Divorce is a terror to children. Maybe that's one reason surfing was so satisfying to me. It was an escape and a medication.

After I barely graduated high school at seventeen years old, I spent two years surfing and dabbled in waiting tables. I worked at Pizza Hut for a while and then Bennigan's, a bar and grill chain. But I had zero responsibilities living with my kind father, who gave me lots of space. We did regularly attend church together with his new wife, Terry, and my stepbrother, Michael. My mother also remarried, to Jim, giving me a stepsister, Renee, and another stepbrother, Brian.

As a teenager at church, in a congregation of a couple of thousand people, I was sure that God was real, because every single week it seemed like that blasted guy in the pulpit was talking specifically to me, with details that he couldn't possibly know about my life. This knowing that God had my number was so pronounced that I literally prayed one time, "Okay God, I hear You calling me to be an Episcopal priest. But I want to be an air traffic controller. Would You please make me an air traffic controller?"

Sure wish I had listened more carefully to that bit in church about not insisting on my own way. Would've saved me a whole bunch of pain, suffering, turmoil and even terror.

IN THE ARMY NOW

When I was 19 years old, all of the responsibility-free life that I was enjoying seemed to come to a natural end. By then my dad had gently prompted me toward college numerous times. I knew I couldn't surf forever. I carried a sense of needing to do something productive with my life, and air traffic control (ATC) was the only thing that held any of my interest.

Believe me, I had zero interest in more school. I evaluated all of the armed services, but the US Army was the only one that would guarantee my training as an air traffic controller. In the Army at that time (late 80s), they actually called it a contract. If you couldn't successfully pass your job training, you were released from the obligation of further service. So that's what I signed up for—Air Traffic Control training.

I left the beach and went to Boot Camp at Ft. McClellan, Alabama, in April 1987. What a change of reality. Our drill instructors were quick to tell us that only the minimum sleep requirements would be given to us. Right away they made it clear that we would not receive more than four hours of sleep per every twenty-four-hour period. The other twenty hours every single day of Boot Camp belonged wholly to our Drill Sergeants. They made good use of them too. We would be awakened with abrasive shouts at 3:00 a.m.

"You have three minutes to be downstairs, in formation, dressed and ready! If 100 percent of you are not downstairs, dressed and ready in formation within three minutes, you will all suffer my wrath!" It was not unusual to have three or four drill instructors barking commands and/or insults at us at the same time. That gave me a new definition to "rude awakening." Well, we didn't have to spend any time fussing with our hair, that's for sure. We were all bald as could be. It was enough time to throw on our combat fatigues and boots, quickly brush our teeth and get downstairs, into formation.

Of course, we suffered our drill instructors' wrath many times: push-ups to no end, sit-ups, running in place and face-to-face standing perfectly still while being showered with spit, emphasizing the points being relentlessly hurled at us.

One morning I was running in strict formation with my company. It was 0'dark-thirty and the whole company ran together in heart, in voice, in step, and in obedience, reverberating whatever the Drill Sergeant said. Actually, the cadences were quite creative and fun, while drilling home the point that we were no longer our own. Now we were the property of the United States government, built strong for its service. I had a second mind of thought as I ran that morning, repeating in cadence, "Way down in the valley, I heard a great roar, it was Charlie Company (us), putting the peddle to the floor, and we won't back down anymore; we pushed them into the river, and laughed when they drowned! Left, left, left, right'll, left!" Running along, I thought, *I'm bald! This is crazy–this is nuts!* Continuing aloud, "Left, left, left, right'll, left, right'll, left…"

It wasn't long before I was all-in and gung-ho. I joined for selfish reasons, but caught the fire of giving all for a united cause, with my brothers right there next to me. I chomped at the bit to go to war and pitied any fool who would confront me. Surfing requires upper-body strength, and the Army took what I had and made it better. I received the Expert Marksmanship qualification with my M-16 and appreciated the fighting techniques that we were taught.

On one 20-mile march through the Appalachian Mountains during Boot Camp we were loaded with heavy backpacks. Miles into an uphill climb with no end in sight at a blistering pace the Drill Instructor barked, "Who thinks this is too hard?"

I thought, *Now is the time to show leadership!*

"I do, Drill Sergeant!" I shouted.

Yeah, that was a mistake. He stopped the march "for a rest"—that is push-ups, running in place, and jumping-jacks with loaded rucksacks. The fellas were not too happy with me, and I chose to quietly follow after that, although the Instructors subsequently made me a squad leader in our platoon.

At the end of that particular march one of our men fell to the ground in convulsions as a result of heat exhaustion and over exertion. As he convulsed we wanted to rush to him, to pour water on him or something. But the Drill Sergeant wouldn't let us, "Let the maggot die if he can't take it! Don't you dare go near him! Let the weakling die!" It was an ugly sight, seeing our fellow soldier foam at the mouth while doing the cockroach shuffle on his back. They ended up marching us off to eat, and about a half hour later we saw him in a bathtub of ice. He ended up washing out of

Boot Camp. Another man intentionally shot his own toe off in an attempt to go home on his own terms. He planned to get himself an honorable discharge on medical grounds, drawing a monthly disability check for the rest of his life. He got busted and was dishonorably discharged instead.

But I made it through Boot Camp and advanced to AIT (Advanced Individual Training) in Ft Rucker, Alabama. This is where each soldier, now fit and ready for war, learned a secondary skill. Yes, it had been drilled into us by then that we were combat-ready troops first. The military discipline of physical training and unity continued daily. And we went to school five days a week. It was the first time in my life that I loved school.

I felt like one of the robots in a *Transformer* movie. A robot sneaks on-board Air Force One and taps into the National Defense system via its on-board computers. As he plugs into the vast database of knowledge, he is thoroughly and completely energized, jacked-up and electrified by what he is receiving, rapidly gobbling it up and totally digesting it to his own delight. That is what aviation school was to me. When the teachers explained how there were highways in the sky, like roads, how they were formed by electronics on the ground that broadcasted radio signals into the air, even creating countless named intersections, how we had to memorize this map in the sky and how specific procedures were required to be followed to the "T" by everyone involved in flight, I plugged into that massive wave, rode its download with elation and never looked back.

Most of the other students in school displayed confusion and difficulty. They were puzzled and had to labor through intricate details of hows, whys, speech-pattern requirements of aviation phraseology, and so on. Some washed out and had to go to other kinds of AIT or were discharged from the military altogether. I ate it up.

My instructor would sit me down in front of a simulated air traffic control scenario with various types of aircraft loaded with troops and equipment, and call other instructors and students to gather around and watch. Then he'd start the there's-no-turning-back clock. When that clock begins, the flights live or die by your command. Yeah, there's pressure in that. I felt the pressure too, but I also had the ability to just dive right in and go with some amazing flow of unspoken knowledge of what was best.

The simulated scenario produces a three-dimensional puzzle that the controller holds in his mind, fitting all of the requirements of priorities together into a certain type of living form, and then reforming it continually as the flow of what's in his mind is translated (or not!) into reality simply through speech. During these simulations, other trainees maneuvered little toy aircraft around a rather goofy miniature airfield according to the controller's commands.

Every aviation-lingo verbal command–and they can get fast and furious–prompts a type of corresponding ATC shorthand marking on small strips of paper called "flight strips," one flight strip per aircraft. Flight strips are a written record of everything going on with the flight from ATC point of view. The controller writes ATC shorthand on the strips while speaking. It's very important to write while speaking, pen and mouth in motion together. This was one of those things that came easy to me, but washed out others.

Over time, as commands are issued, each flight strip begins to tell the story of its associated flight's activity while that flight was being moved around, from start to finish—every turn given, every speed change, every change of altitude—every spoken thing, and then some. Things move fast. An issued command has to be recorded as the picture flows. We would need to keep our eyes on the flights while splitting our attention to place our hand in the right spot to make our mark on the respective strip. And it's all got to be done exactly right.

Making these shorthand-type marks on flight strips as you go makes it possible for another controller to provide assistance if necessary. For example, if a controller has a heart attack while working air traffic, another controller could step up, examine the cardiac victim's flight strips and develop his own mental picture and magic plan to solve it all, while others tend to the incapacitated controller. The flight strips also create a retainable, official record for examination at a later date if needed (i.e., a disaster investigation).

We combine all the flight strips, representing many aircraft, for marking and managing air traffic scenarios, corporately displaying a picture of reality in the sky. Just when you think you were on the cusp of having an exact match in mind and matter, an unforeseen emergency arises, and your entire picture, with its priorities, must immediately be reformed. Again and again and again this flow unfolded during training. To complicate matters, they would occasionally remove the goofy miniature airfield representation to leave the air traffic controller working with mind, pencil, flight strips, clock and microphone only. It was quite normal for trainees to get up from the hot seat (the control position) with sweat rings under their arms after a mere thirty-minute scenario.

After a given simulation, one instructor asked me, "You've spent time on the radio before, haven't you?" I had not.

I don't know how or why it all made such good sense to me, it just did. At graduation best students were selected from each class as Honor Graduates. The proof that I ate up air traffic control school like a starving person introduced to a buffet is that the official government records correctly reflect I was chosen to be the "Distinguished Honor Graduate," the best student out of multiple classes, in all aspects of soldiering too, not only scholastics.

After graduation, where in the whole wide world would I be deployed? Now I had the skills to go into combat and control air traffic anywhere. Korea? That was a destination for many good troops. Germany? This was before the Berlin Wall came down, so that was a possibility too. I didn't know where on the planet the Army would send me, and I was their investment now.

Orders came forth for Ft Polk, LA, just two states from my ATC school. I checked into the military base in Louisiana with about sixty other soldiers from all over America. Each soldier needed to be issued his personal combat gear, determined by his specialty of training. All were given an inventory sheet and duffle bag to progress through an inventory line. Some, depending on their trade, were even given two duffle bags to fill with combat gear. I pitied those guys.

I noticed that the other air traffic controllers with me were given an inventory sheet that was much longer than mine. We progressed through the line together, and again and again they were given things that were not given to me, filling their duffle bags full all the way to the top. I finished the line with less than half of a duffle bag worth of military gear and a distinguishing piece of combat apparatus, one I saw no other soldier receive: aviator's sunglasses! Genuine, government-issued aviation sunglasses.

Are you serious? Awesome! I thought.

Many of the real soldiers sneered at me, comparing their heavy duffle bags with my "combat gear."

My ATC friends were assigned to the aviation combat unit on base, while I was sent to the civilian-operated airfield (DOD, or the Department of Defense) with its ATC tower at Ft. Polk Army Airfield. I was graciously welcomed and then assigned to the tutelage of the well-known toughest trainer there, MX (after the "baddest" weapon of his era, the MX missile). He welcomed me under his wing by giving me a double-edged nickname, Ace. He was mocking my inexperience, giving minimal weight to my graduate honors, while promising his ability to "bring me up right." All of the controllers at Polk Army Airfield were civilians, except for a few like me. We were the young, inexperienced guys being trained by retired US Air Force controllers or other civilians who were on distinct courses to further their ATC careers. Anyone there who wasn't retired Air Force had their hearts set to work air traffic in the FAA (Federal Aviation Administration)–the big leagues.

I advanced from ATC school simulations to keying up the microphone and directing actual pilots of varying types of aircraft. It was such a rush to mix the aircraft sitting still on the runway (waiting for clearance to take off, for example) with the ones in the sky that were coming or going at speeds from 120 to 250 mph. I began shooting gaps between airborne aircraft, mixing and merging flights, applying the minimum separation standards, and learning how to flex my voice to impart an authority that was clearly understood by my listeners as an instruction to be heeded. The control of being "the man" (really, the law) wasn't bad either. In the air traffic control environment, no flight does anything without first being told to do so, from changing air speed to turning left or right to climbing or descending and beyond. The controller is in charge.

It turned out that at Polk Army Airfield when I completed my training to work on my own I received an FAA issued Control Tower Operator (CTO) certificate. Any FAA credential is golden to those who aspire to join the most elite ATC agency on the planet. To actually hold an FAA issued ATC credential while being in the military was rare. Over time, I would learn that not many who attempted to get into the big leagues of ATC would actually make it in the FAA. The washout rate was drastic. Having these credentials by the age of twenty was a significant head start for me. The FAA knew my name, and had declared me as one of their own by issuing the credential before I even got out of military service. A rare occurrence. Indeed, I felt like I was "the man."

Air traffic control has a reputation for being high in stress. But to me stress brings a negative connotation, and ATC wasn't stress. For me it was a rush, like catching just the right bone-crushing wave. And like in surfing, if I messed up, I was going to get hurt. The ATC parallel was the consideration that other people's lives and my government's money were in my hands. It would be crushing to screw that up. But if I didn't mess up, I was going to enjoy it. So for me it was more intense than stressful. I loved the energy and penetrating rush of the vast responsibility, control and success, all moving at blazing aviation speeds with potential for disaster at any second. I thrived on being in charge.

During the time I was in training and being challenged under MX's scrutiny, I wasn't bored. But shortly after becoming certified and working on my own, I longed for more. More adrenaline, more excitement.

It wasn't long before I extended my rush by flirting with disaster outside of work. I began seeking pleasures by drinking, partying, and chasing skirts. At the time I rationalized that I was celebrating the success I had earned. I still shrink in humiliation at how I could claim to be so sharp and smart while being so dull and stupid at the same time. Eventually, I actually got thrown out of my cushy tower assignment and deployed with the tactical ATC unit (the real soldiers) on base for having inappropriate relations with the civilian tower chief's daughter. Ace found his kicks in the gamble, but got caught holding a losing hand. The nickname became history, but I retained my FAA credentials through it all, so I wasn't too broken up about it.

I was now in the tactical unit with more of a focus on combat, but I still wasn't content. One weekend I drove from Louisiana to Texas for a Joan Jett concert and returned to base late for duty. The military placed me on barracks restriction; I was grounded. I could go to work and to my room, and that was it. Unwilling to deny my need for risk and the rush that came with it, I snuck out on a Friday night and drove a couple of hours to a dance club in Lake Charles, Louisiana.

I hadn't been there more than twenty minutes when a hot little black-haired, big-hazel-eyed girl came up to me. We started talking and we danced (although rhythm is an enigma to me). I didn't get in trouble that night. I made it back to the base undetected, but I couldn't get the girl out of my mind. Ultimately I ended up with a wife!

Susan has a rich French heritage, growing up in the tiny seaside (well, the Gulf of Mexico), fishing town of Cameron, Louisiana. Her family culture is altogether Cajun. She was eighteen when I met her and her Cajun world was about all she knew of life. Her grandmother didn't speak English and French was a required subject for all of the students in the elementary school in the town where she grew up. I saw fishing, shrimping, family, and celebration. I fell in love with her, her culture, and the Cajun food certainly captured me too.

We shared a similar background in that her parents divorced when she was nine. I'm a couple of years older than she, so our parents divorced at roughly the same time. It did not escape me that she and my sister endured divorce at the same age and time. In fact, there seemed to be a whole Mr. Worldly Knight in shining armor has come to rescue the country damsel in the air about our meeting. Like me, she had bounced between living with her mother and father until she graduated from high school. Then she lived with her dad and stepmother, attending McNeese State University in Lake Charles when I met her.

After three months of driving back and forth to Lake Charles from Ft. Polk and running up crazy phone bills with my newly found, satisfying rush of Cajun-spice, I asked her father for her hand in marriage and we officially came together on July 4, 1989. Breathtaking fireworks became our matrimonial portion.

A Justice of the Peace performed our ceremony in a gazebo out in a country field. Her family bought us clothes for the event. They attended and then arranged a reception in a small town hall. There we received a couple of laundry basketfuls of groceries, a cooler full of shark-steaks, pots and pans, sheets, towels, and the like. We moved into a small apartment just outside of the Army base and began learning how to live together and be married.

Seven months later in February 1990, having saved up two-month's leave for an early release, I was honorably discharged from the Army. Prior to my discharge I took the ATC entrance exam for the FAA, an exam that was dreaded by candidates nationwide. This exam chewed up applicants and spit them out, their hopes and dreams with them. It wasn't good enough to just pass the test. Many would scrape by with a passing score of 70 to 89 only to realize that such a poor result excluded them from even being considered. To have any chance whatsoever of entering the agency, one needed to get at least a 90 on the exam. My score of 94, combined with holding an FAA issued CTO certificate, brought my dream of working air traffic professionally ever closer to becoming a reality. I had put in my job application for the FAA just prior to leaving the military. Having been discharged without yet hearing back from the agency left us in limbo.

While waiting to hear back from the FAA, we moved back to Florida and in with my mother. I was so glad to be out of the military, married, and returning to the beach. I could resume my daily rush of catching waves, even while trying to catch my dream of riding all the way to the top of the FAA.

The ATC application process included all sorts of follow-ups, check-ins, promptings and prodding from my end. I think I may have even harassed the government for the job. The hiring of a federal employee at the time threw the applicant into a quagmire of bureaucrats who didn't seem to know one another or how they were supposed to work together. I wasn't about to allow someone else's confusion to keep me from my dream. My "job" became coordinating, communications, and pressing, pressing, pressing. This work only required a couple of hours per day, so after making my calls to the government I would hit the beach to surf for a few hours. Then I'd shove my board onto the fully reclined front passenger's seat of our Chevy Cavalier and drive to pick up my sweet hotty-wife who was working as a teller at a bank. She would change into her swimming suit in the backseat, peeling off her dress, stockings and heels, readying herself for sand, sun, and sea while I returned us both to the beach. I was living a dream come true, while seeking the greater wave of my professional dream.

Sometimes Susan would bring a camera to take pictures of me riding waves, but she preferred combing the beach for sharks' teeth. It wasn't long before she became an expert at finding them and amassed a large, nice collection of various sizes, types, and colors. I surfed, she hunted for treasures, things we both loved. Life was presenting itself as fun, quite carefree, and totally easy, but I had so much invested in the desire to be an air traffic controller that each day of waiting to hear what I wanted to hear seemed like an unjust delay. Looking back, I think I carried an unnecessary weight regarding our future.

As the waters began to grow too cold to surf, in October 1990, I finally received a hire letter in the mail from the FAA. I got my dream job! And my first assignment was to San Juan, Puerto Rico. My dream come true would even begin in the Caribbean. The letter instructed me to report for duty on November 17, 1990, at the San Juan CERAP (Combined Enroute Radar Approach Control). I was stepping up from the control tower operator function to a higher-paying and more challenging radar controller environment.

Susan and I anticipated our relocation to Puerto Rico as if we were embarking upon an extended honeymoon. For the month prior to reporting for duty, we lived in utter elation. Our future lay before us, brilliant and full of promise. I had just turned twenty-three and she was twenty. Our first day on the island delivered us straight into reality.

THE BIG LEAGUES: PUSHING TIN

At first San Juan was just as we had imagined. The smell of the ocean was carried upon its breeze, sweeping over the entire airport area. Tall palm trees and high-rise condominiums lined the beach.

The CERAP arranged for a taxi to pick us up and take us to a hotel. Shortly after exiting the airport, the taxi-driver raced the wrong way down a clearly marked one-way street. When I voiced my concern, he replied in Spanish. Neither of us knew any Spanish. Gauging our panic, he then replied in broken English, "Don't worry, there's plenty of room for us to go in this direction!" Our Puerto Rico adventure had begun.

Our first abode was a penthouse apartment in a condominium set upon volcanic rock in Luquillo near the east end of the island. From our balcony we could see numerous Caribbean islands, including the US Virgin Island of St. Thomas. And from our front door we had an awesome view of America's only national tropical rain forest, El Yunque, set in the mountains only a couple of minutes' drive from our front door. Much to my delight, our condo sat right on the beach of the famed Puerto Rican surfing spot known as The Wall, and I didn't waste any time at all splashing right into the super clear waters. From our balcony I could watch the sets come in. I was totally captivated by the beauty of seeing the ocean floor through the incoming waves. When the sight became too much to bear, I would grab my board and get busy with it.

The penthouse was a nice way to ease into our extended honeymoon. However, the only way to get to our condo required driving through a small, poverty-stricken town, past dirty plywood structures as homes and businesses, starving dogs roaming wild, and freshly slaughtered pigs hanging in the open air, being swarmed by insects. The poverty was an arresting shock to us.

Sometimes we took day long drives to tour the island, and spent the night out on the island. The mountaintop views of the ocean also included other islands as well as the profound poverty around us. Going home through the large electronic iron gate guarding the condo reminded us that we were exceptionally fortunate, but also brought a certain sense of sobriety regarding our security. We were no doubt minorities in a foreign land.

Other than that, the culture provided pretty much anything a young couple could possibly want to do, from water sports to dining out and dancing, mountain adventures and then some. We hiked through the mountainous tropical rain forest, El Yunque, visiting secluded waterfalls. On the way to the national rain forest, or on the way home, we would stop for pinchos (bite-sized portions of pork on a skewer, grilled) and coconut milk straight out of coconuts with their tops lopped off. We drove to remote beaches like the famed spot, Rin Con, meaning "little corner [of the island]" to spend the night, so that I could surf. We also took all-inclusive day-sails to uninhabited islands with white sandy beaches and crystal clear waters.

My commute into San Juan every day took me about an hour. The drive and culture felt nothing less to me than the Wild Wild West. Being a hot shot in my early 20s made that environment a pretty good fit, as it grew on me. It was not unusual to see a police officer directing traffic on a hot day in the middle of the road while holding and enjoying a cold beer. As I drove by I'd lift a pseudo, island-made Heineken and "Salud!" with one hand while holding the steering wheel with the other.

Sidewalks were not off limits to vehicles, if you deemed it necessary. Drivers carried the same lax attitude toward rules and regulations as the police force (most of whom were "on the take"). It was well known that the corruption ran straight up and throughout the whole of the government. Bags of US mail were routinely found discarded in rivers when the postal workers deemed it "necessary" to take the day off. It wasn't long before I realized the only law I needed to adhere to was going to bed alive at night.

One early Sunday morning shortly after sunrise on the way to work I came upon a clogged-up street. Cars were parked throughout the street and alongside the road, and pedestrians crowded the road and sides of the road too. I needed to get to work and became aggravated because I couldn't get through the congestion. We had purchased a small island-type car for maneuverability, so I started honking my horn and crept, crawled, edged, and wiggled my way forward inch by inch. As I got near the head of the disturbance, what I saw stunned me into silence. It was a hanging. The public had lynched someone on the side of the road. I slipped through unscathed, retreating to my US Government secured facility. I found comfort in the red and white sign on the fence next to the guard shack where we entered the compound, "Attention! Interrupting the service of this facility may result in death and shall be prosecuted by the United States of America." Frankly, I think it was saying not to mess with what we were doing there, that interruptions could kill the people we were serving, but I liked to think it meant the armed guards would shoot anyone who interfered with our peace. I suppose I was lying to myself, but in light of real Puerto Rican terrorists, who successfully struck the US Air National Guard there and regularly caused massive, island-wide electricity blackouts, it was a comfort I willingly chose to believe.

The air traffic control facility operated inside its own building and was connected to the regional administration building via a covered, open-air walkway. Both buildings had a traditional "federal" look, while set within an authentically tropical and meticulously manicured, fenced-in compound. Radarscopes filled a large control room, similar to typical scenes on TV of a NASA control room. Large satellite dishes, one with a huge red lightning bolt painted across it, sat like big watchdogs on the tropical and manicured, high-fenced-in property. I found this all just right for where I was in my heart and life. I was home at the condo, on the beach, or at work.

My assignment at the San Juan CERAP began with the requirement to memorize the facility's airspace, the roadmap in the sky. An aviation chart for any big league radar facility looks like someone threw a bowl of spaghetti noodles into the air and took a picture of it. Each "noodle" represents an airway, a road in the sky, and has a name. The sky roads are derived from points in the sky or broadcasted by navigational aids from the ground. Each intersection, the point of intersecting noodles, also has a specific five-letter name. And there are areas within the mumble-jumble that are special-use airspace, like specially reserved military-only areas and areas for only the DEA to operate and…well, legally I can say no more. Spy planes have to fly somewhere. All the mumble-jumble creates corridors or tunnels of airspace too. The sky picture is so complex that the overall airspace is divvied up between many controllers within the facility's overall airspace, although we each had to memorize the entire picture.

With my upgraded responsibilities, the speeds of my air traffic increased from 120-250 mph to 180–500 mph. I likened it to "shooting gaps," mixing and merging varying types of aircraft with their respective varying speeds and applying minimum separation standards. I would picture a moving gap between two moving objects, then "shoot" that gap by placing another moving object right in the center of the first two moving objects. As controller I had control of all three objects. In other words, I could slow the back guy, speed the leading guy and cram the third guy in the middle—forcing a gap to shoot. Ah, but doing so would affect the entire rest of the picture, the other twenty aircraft. What an adrenaline rush! It was wild, fast, and furious. Also I had to reserve corridors and classified portions of the sky in some places, reducing the amount of available airspace. These invisible corridors were like three-dimensional tunnels in the sky. Their unseen walls, ceilings and floors were not to be violated, or death could occur. When working air traffic you are doing all sorts of things at once, from looking and speaking to the planes on your scope to coordinating with other facilities on the landlines to pointing out relevant information to the guy sitting next to you, and more.

Applying minimum separation standards means that flights were not allowed to get too close to one another. But look, a good air traffic controller won't let them get too far apart either. That would be wasting airspace! No. The object is to run them as tight as you can without letting them get too close. At the minimum separation standard the aircraft were safe from smacking into one another, but if that standard were violated, two planes could go from five miles apart to a mid-air collision in about twenty seconds. So for the rest of my career I worked in an environment in which air traffic could go from safe to collision in less than half a minute. Yeah, time to be on your toes.

To pass this initial phase of training, reporting to the CERAP, one would be given a blank sheet of paper, a pencil and a ruler, and required to draw and label the airspace map from memory without references and without error. That might sound strict, but within all of our training, contingencies were being built in to cope with unforeseen trouble. For instance, if the radarscope were to become inoperative, the controller still had a brain and the minimum tools needed—a pencil, flight strips, a clock and a microphone—to get the job done. And he had to, because thousands of lives were in his hands. Everyone in the air would be without a clue as to any FAA equipment failure. In such an event, the only picture a controller would have of the sky would be formulated in his head. The flight strips come in very handy in such a real scenario. It happened to me on many occasions.

The agency built in maximum time frames, too, for us to work any given session within our eight-hour shift. It was not legal to keep a controller "plugged in" to a section of airspace (sector) for more than two hours at a time during any shift of work. Ideally, a controller would work traffic for thirty to forty-five minutes and then take a thirty minute break, rotating through different sectors throughout his eight to ten hour shift. In San Juan, far away from the mainland, that two-hour limit was routinely violated. It was by no means acceptable to violate the minimum separation standards between aircraft, but it was normal practice to violate the maximum allowable time-frame set for controllers to stay focused.

A group of about a half dozen of us arrived at the CERAP together to form a class of newbies. We studied together, learning about our new airspace and the radar equipment we would be working on. San Juan was sort of the armpit of the agency, along with Guam and other remote locations, and was given old and antiquated equipment. Its airspace extended in a 250-mile radius from San Juan, encompassing most of the Caribbean, with a 500-mile diameter. For instance, St. Thomas was on my radarscope. St. Martin was on my scope. Haiti, St. Kitts and so on, all depicted on my radar screen. Beyond our radar view San Juan's airspace also included some air traffic airspace that is rather rare and certainly intentionally avoided by the vast majority of air traffic controllers. It is referred to as "non-radar, oceanic airspace." This is where planes fly under control of ATC without any visual aid on our part whatsoever. Just like it sounds, non-radar, and too far from any tower or other method of sight. In the non-radar ATC environment, controllers use their mind and flight strips only, along with two-way communications to the pilots and a clock to decipher speeds, distances, etc. This exceedingly challenging work environment is responsible for washing out many an air traffic controller.

After passing the initial memorization training, we were sent to the control room floor. Each of us was assigned to a specific trainer to begin training in the non-radar airspace. The idea was to use the non-radar environment to weed out the less skilled controllers before they even got a chance to sit in front of a radarscope.

The massive airspace is divided up into countless quadrants, if you will, called "sectors." The aspiration is to work under the intense scrutiny of your trainer, who is ultimately responsible for the lives at hand, until he says you are ready to work on your own. At that point, another seasoned veteran controller with special training for the task would sit and watch you work air traffic, evaluating how well you performed. If this evaluation, or "check ride" as we would call it, went well, you were certified to work on your own and received a pay raise too. Obviously, new controllers were eager to certify on as many sectors as they could. Within my first year on the job, I enjoyed numerous $10,000 pay raises. As was my pattern, I became increasingly energized and pumped up by the work, raring and ready to feed on more intensity. I quickly certified on all assigned sectors and became a trainer and an evaluator, receiving extra pay for training and grading others. I was fully submerged in my element, like a fish in water. I would work air traffic with life-critical things going on all over the place, multitasking to the max, and having just enough time to take in a full breath. In the midst of the high demand one day, overflowing with adrenaline, I lifted my head, looked straight up, and shouted, "I do this job for the glory!" It was busy as all get-out, and I separated myself for the tiniest moment to shout with exhilaration. I had made it to my goal; I was riding the wave of ATC. Shredding it would be more like it. I was tearing it up, just like I did when I caught one of my beloved ocean waves.

Part of the multitasking of ATC includes numerous pilots regularly calling on different frequencies at the same time. They can't hear one another broadcasting, but the controller has no way to separate the multiple transmissions. To an untrained or unskilled ear, it sounds like a bunch of unintelligible garble. But somehow I could discern what was going on and then prioritize needs and commands to move airliners ("pushing tin") with maximum efficiency. In front of that radarscope, I'd have an earpiece plugged into my ear—as if the entire airspace with its speedy fluency was plugged into my mind—and the microphone boom at my mouth, my finger on the trigger to key the mic, and I'd be broadcasting on up to ten different frequencies, like radio channels, at the same time. One frequency would cover the northwest quadrant of the radarscope, another frequency the north part, another one the northeast and so on. In addition, I had some thirty landlines, or instant telephone communications, with my coworkers.

Sitting there at the radarscope in San Juan, I had a direct line to New York, a direct line to Miami, a direct line to Santa Domingo all the way around the Caribbean, and direct lines to other air traffic controllers inside and outside of the building. While working live air traffic, if I pushed a landline button it would go "hot" to another controller. That means I spoke directly into whatever he was doing without his needing to answer the call. So I could push the button and say, for instance, "Miami, San Juan on the six two," (the name of that particular line). While the guy in Miami is working traffic, he would hear my voice over a loud speaker, answering as soon as he could for coordination of a myriad of matters. For example, "Delta 123 is having engine problems and needs special handling." Or, sure enough, "My wife is on American 123–don't screw it up!"

I certified as a Full Performance Level (FPL) controller in minimum time, meaning there was nowhere else to train me. Although I won the respect of my co-workers, I'm not going to say it was all gravy. They had issued me one hell of a trainer. More than once after a session of working under his incessant, intentionally overbearing scrutiny, I retreated to a private area to cry. You see, while training, it was not uncommon to have to endure severe abrasiveness from your trainer, even verbal abuse. Some smacking on the back of the head, too. We tolerated this, understanding that our trainers were piling pressure on us so that when we were on our own we would not cave under the pressure of who knows what could and will happen. Those "who knows" were unfathomable, real and imminent. The controller must be able to not only cope with the unforeseen, sometimes crazy, things that certainly come down the pike, but they must do it well while tending to everyone else in the sky. Without fault or error.

I saw and had to work through some exceptionally difficult occurrences during my tenure in San Juan. Severe air turbulence is defined as the pilot's inability to control the aircraft, even with hundreds of people on board, due to weather phenomenon. It's hard to keep a flight in such a state from hitting another airplane, especially when you are successfully doing what you aspire to do, running them consistently tightly together. Sometimes when this dangerous type of air turbulence hit, people did die. If you are not wearing your seatbelt on a commercial flight and your aircraft hits this extraordinary type of turbulence, your head becomes nothing more than a squished orange on the ceiling of the cabin. Physics gives no special treatment to humans, and we are talking about ridiculous conditions of physics (500 mph, etc.). People died. Babies died. And it gets worse. Extreme air turbulence is when the airframe of the aircraft begins to fail. This means the airplane, commercial airliner or not, starts to suffer airframe damage or literally come to pieces in the sky.

As if that's not enough, there are all sorts of other disastrous events that were par for the course. I worked more than one hijacking. I saw planes crash and every soul on board die, more than once. I saw other controllers lose their minds, pilots fail to adequately perform their tasks, aircraft maintenance failures, radarscopes cop out at the worst of times and, as one of the total losses, a microburst that smashed one of my commercial flights straight into the ground, killing everyone. I saw a photo of that particular incident later, and it showed a crash that looked like a pancake.

This is why we were willing to endure ludicrous pressure from our trainers. Once on our own, we were required to cope with anything that happened while continuing to do the job for all of the other people who were still in the sky.

Just because passengers don't hear of all of these troubles doesn't mean they aren't there. We would work thousands of flights per week and these types of incidents were what the odds produced. And frankly, back then, covering up scary incidents was simply part of the FAA culture. If it could be swept under the rug, it was. Even if we air traffic controllers wanted to file a report because of some safety violation or close call, back then management would squash it in a heartbeat if they knew there was no way anyone but the controller could prove it. This created dangerous friction, even hatred, between controllers, who intimately took the public's safety seriously and distant managers who "flew desks" and didn't want the boat rocked by safety compromises that were inconvenient. They wanted nothing unsightly to take place on their watch.

There were countless shifts when crazy things in the sky or in the control room happened so fast that I didn't even have time to fully comprehend the gravity of it all…until after work. I'd grab a few beers for the drive home and after continuing the rush on the Wild Wild West roads of Puerto Rico, be sitting safe and sound at home when flashbacks would begin hitting me, "Whoa! That really happened? Dang, that was so close! I can't believe nobody died (or, it's so sad that they died that way)." Another big swig of alcohol. In the 90s, the Caribbean had the third-highest aviation fatality rate on earth, after Africa and India.

Susan was always wonderful to me. From shoulder rubs to finely prepared meals to physical intimacies, she was eager to please. Sometimes she would join me at work to sit and watch. She said that she thought of each voice she heard, those pilots I directed, as representing hundreds of lives. That's true too. One pilot's voice on the ATC frequency carried scores or hundreds of souls on board. She couldn't understand how air traffic controllers could settle what to do with such finality, just as quickly as they received the masses of information. But it's just the way our minds work. Good air traffic controllers are a unique breed.

Incidentally, the ATC vocation has a disproportionate number of left-handed people, about half of the workforce. That's way lop-sided compared to society at large. I'm left-handed too. And, the presidents of the United States in the last thirty to forty years also demonstrate a lop-sided proportion of left-handed people, in an even greater percentage than the ATC workforce. Before forty years ago, it was considered a shame in our society to be left-handed, so who knows how accurate the presidential records are before that.

The movie *Pushing Tin* with John Cusack, Cate Blanchett, Billy Bob Thornton and Angelina Jolie does a fine job of depicting the culture of air traffic controllers. Overall, respectfully, because I am a fan of all four of those artists, I think the movie is quite vulgar and not very good. However, *Pushing Tin* has the most accurate portrayal of how we lived and worked that I've ever seen in a movie. Even in the opening moments of the film, it depicts a controller (John Cusack) working traffic while chanting "sugarless gum, sugarless gum, sugarless gum," in between the moments of keying the microphone to broadcast complex instructions. The mind is fully engaged with a complex and fluent puzzle, and so jacked-up on adrenaline at the same time that even in the idle moments it can't be still or quiet. Long term, this can't be good for the human personality. I worked with guys who spontaneously quacked like ducks at each other while working air traffic. Some controllers had profound facial tics. I couldn't hold a conversation with them without thinking, *This dude is wacked!*

Guys who worked elbow to elbow didn't always get along. Occasionally fights broke out, like when one of the guys kept reaching his arm into his coworker's space to point out relevant flight information on his screen. There'd be so much alpha-male going on during these physical altercations that air traffic control sectors and responsibilities would be abandoned. Other controllers would do their best to keep the public safe by jumping in on the deserted sectors while trying to keep up with their own. Yeah, it was wild, like the island.

Management would turn their heads the other way, to avoid seeing all of the overt craziness that took place every day. The traffic was being worked though–that's what mattered to them. Oh, it was crazy, but the air traffic was being worked.

HEADING OFF-RADAR

Susan and I were fortunate we could get away and enjoy island travels wherever we wanted to go in the Caribbean. Showing my FAA ID granted me free flights and even special treatment with the different large and small airlines. They didn't know if I might be an FAA inspector and were sure to treat me well. Flights to adjacent islands were not expensive, so we could buy Susan's tickets for cheap. So for years on my days off we island hopped to both famous and largely unknown tropical islands—from St. Thomas (U.S.V.I.) to Palominitos (Puerto Rican) to St. Johns (U.S.V.I.) to St. Marteen (half French and clothing optional, half Dutch), to St. Barts (French) to Anguilia (British Overseas Territory) to Virgin Gorda (BVI, British Virgin Island) and beyond.

We went where our young, honeymoon-empowered hearts wanted to go. With clothes, without clothes, with booze, without booze. We did what we wanted and enjoyed one another and the setting we had worked to obtain. You'd think someone in such a situation would have nothing to complain about or any desire to ever leave the Caribbean.

But the cultural differences of the Puerto Rican Wild

West grew tiresome and heavy. I endured more than one close call with death. One morning on the way to work, another driver sped through a red light and I t-boned him at 55 mph. My hands, firmly gripping the steering wheel right before impact, tore the wheel off of the column, which then heart-punched me at impact. While I gasped for air but couldn't find the ability to breathe, marauders rushed to me and plundered me and my vehicle. No assistance was offered at all.

I eventually crawled to the side of the road to avoid further disaster until an ambulance with only wood benches in back finally arrived to take me to the hospital. I was able to breathe shallowly by then, and called Susan on the cell phone to come and get me. She took me to the US Naval base, where I received emergency, compassionate care. But that wasn't before the doctors at the Puerto Rican hospital injected something into my arm. I saw the bottle label the injection was drawn from and told the Naval doctor about it. He laughed, saying, "They gave you a local anesthetic in your arm!" Sure enough, my upper arm where I received the shot was numb, while the rest of me remained in excruciating pain.

We endured racism many, many times. In the work environment, fellow employees who were Puerto Rican would intentionally speak Spanish about American people right around them, to conceal their conversation and mock them. It didn't take me long to understand Spanish, so I knew what they were saying, and what they were doing, although I never let them know. Susan suffered intense sexism at grocery stores and the like. Once when she asked a manager of a grocery store where the Margarita mix was, he mocked her as if she were speaking Russian. One time a major hurricane was bearing down upon the island and as everyone sprang into panic-buying of supplies, we found that all the stores had been emptied of the necessities. Clean drinking water was being sold on the side of the road, and a large crowd was pressing upon the sellers with no line or organization whatsoever. Susan and I eventually managed to get ourselves through the crowd and up close to the seller. As we opened our mouths to voice our desired purchase, he barked, "*No agua for gringos aqui!* Away! Away!" (No water for American's here! Away! Away!) He turned from us and toward the locals next to us to sell them water. This was our undeniable experience during our time in Puerto Rico in the 1990s, right before the US military pulled out of the island.

Not all the locals were that way. It seemed a 50-50 venture. Half loved the USA and wanted to become a state, and the other half hated us and seemed to prefer our death to our departure from the island. There didn't seem to be any locals who were in between those two extremes. This meant that gringos had to remain on their toes at all times when in public. We survived the hurricane by approaching an agreeable neighbor, giving her money, and having her purchase what we needed. That storm sounded like a miles long train, thunderously rolling across our roof for hours on end. The power went out for weeks, but we survived.

At work, I routinely suffered gross injustices in the air traffic control environment. The hostility between controllers and management continued to fester. I had stepped into an ongoing intense friction, even hatred. The managers wanted a quiet operation. The [admittedly proud] controllers wanted everything to be perfect—for safety, and for the sake of honoring their sacrifices to do things right. As if, "What? I'm required to be perfect and work ATC perfectly…while you managers let glaring faults grow into total calamities (equipment, procedures, etc.)" Controllers felt abused and overlooked. Managers often demonstrated that they were afraid to work traffic. Many managers were washouts and had obtained their positions through politics, to put it politely, and we certainly used their weakness in this regard as leverage to torment them. Sassy? Yes, an understatement. Recall that this conflict is what caused former President Reagan to mass-fire controllers in the 80s. He would have fit into the management side of this friction, much as I admire him today. It's true that we controllers were like divas. That contributed to the mass firing.

Management shot back by deeming controllers as whiners and they retaliated every chance they found. Furthermore, many times they would deliberately ignore warnings because a controller raised the issue, rather than management. It was as if air traffic controllers were an undesirable thorn in the side of management, who demonstrated an attitude of, "If we could only get this mission done without those pesky air traffic controllers." All the while moms, dads, babies, business folks, saints, and the like were upheld and kept safely in the air by the grace of God.

On one particular occasion, I was working two sectors. There was no controller sitting next to me at the time, because the airspace-sectors had been combined onto my scope. I noticed water from the ceiling dripping onto the large electronic device (radarscope) right next to me, raising concern that I might get fried if the water was allowed to continue dripping. I pointed it out to the distant manager at his desk, and he promptly ignored me. I pointed it out again, verbally bemoaning his neglect—all the while working traffic. Again, he lowered his head to look away from me and toward his paperwork. Finally, I began counting down, as if to announce when the heavy, wet, two-foot by four-foot ceiling tile was going to collapse from the very high control room ceiling, "Ten! Nine! Eight!. . . ." Yes, I was being obnoxious toward the manager who thought that my safety concern was a bother. After counting down from ten two or three times, the ceiling tile became overloaded with water and came crashing down onto the scope next to me. There was a flash of bright light and the machine went black, rendering it useless. From his desk the manager nonchalantly picked up the phone and called for a maintenance crew. They came and removed that hundreds of thousands of dollars-worth piece of equipment that was now totally ruined and replaced it with another.

The agency had its dirt but I was no angel either. I drank heavily and frequently. Anyone could stop at "illegal" (most were protected by the police) drug-points at a myriad of places along the drive from San Juan to the east end of the island where we lived. And I did. I began by using a little bit of pot and it did seem to help me, with the flashbacks and such. I didn't seem to suffer any adverse effects the next day either, like drinking a lot of alcohol would cause. I think that here my gifting to perform ATC actually worked against me. Believe it or not, I failed to be challenged by work after just two years. I knew I needed to keep my head clear, so I wouldn't drink or smoke prior to work, unlike some of the other controllers or pilots.

But then eventually I tried cocaine. Wow. Talk about a rush, and seemingly ATC performance enhancing. I would go for a few months using this new buzz and then check myself by discontinuing its use for a few months, to avoid a serious chemical dependency. In light of the overall chaos of the work environment, my wild behavior of drug use did not stick out like a sore thumb, but was actually par for the course. My whole life was like the Wild Wild West. Everything was lawless, except me plugged into an ATC sector. There I was the law. And the only law, apart from the requirement to go to bed alive at night. I don't justify my bad behavior, but relay just how unsettled reality was. I banked on the public's perception of ATC work as permission to be wild. "Oh, that job is so stressful!" "Yes, it is," is how I responded, using that justification to do what I wanted. I wasn't blind to co-workers and pilots, either, as we hung around with one another. I would often meet with pilots and co-workers at specific bars in discreet places. Bar owners gladly welcomed us because our crowd brought in ridiculous amounts of sales and tips. I didn't party alone. We were a bunch of speed-racers, living large, wild, and free.

(As I share all of these things, please realize that I am speaking of past events. I am describing days gone by, without any personal knowledge of what is taking place in the aviation industry today.)

I began keeping secrets from Susan, money and "powder" secrets. It hindered our personal time together, and I do believe, married and in love as we were, our hearts began to drift away from one another because of my cocaine use and post-work activities. We had been total contentment for one another, but I allowed my heart to begin drifting away and I suppose hers followed, drifting away from me. She became consumed with arts and crafts at home. And we also bought three Miniature-Dachshunds (Bobby, Charlie, and Sandy), to be stand-in children. We wanted to have children, but not in Puerto Rico. Susan loved the puppies and took radical care of them. Our home must have been the most decorated home on the whole island too, with her constant painting and crafting. It was very beautiful.

Each of us was storing hopes and dreams in an unnamed place of our hearts, searching for perfect contentment but never finding deep-down satisfaction with what we had, even island hopping with a hundred grand per year. We were living a wild and wide-open lifestyle, making good money and enjoying favor here and there in all of our endeavors. Susan didn't use any drugs but did enjoy alcohol. There were crazy parties, attended by my co-workers and pilots, at homes on the beach or restaurants or remote locations. I was using whatever I wanted however I wanted. Although I still wasn't drinking on duty like some of the other guys, I wasn't shying away from the powder.

I felt like I couldn't bombard Susan with the fury of the injustices and ineptness I dealt with each day at work, or constantly pile upon her the razor sharp line between life and death that I routinely walked; that didn't seem right to me. After being in Puerto Rico for nearly five years, I began to burn out. Meaning, I wasn't fulfilled; I felt drained and not motivated to improve. I bounced between one mundane shift of work, regardless of its wide array of crazy emergencies, and subsequent parties, from one supposedly exciting event to another not-quite satisfying event. I had been demoralized by management's lack of care for what was right or wrong in the work place. In a sense, they had won. I had learned that instead of insisting on what was right, I should just shut up and push tin. I'm not blaming them, ultimately, for my loose actions. I chose to do what I did. The lure of no-no's was too appealing as another irresistible thrill, and I indulged them as an escape from the intolerable negligence constantly demonstrated by those in charge at work, maybe even a distorted way to strike back at them.

We were both tired of living in "paradise" and longed to return to America. But now, as much as FAA management didn't like me, I was an invaluable asset to the control-room floor. Once certified as an FPL, you were a hot and difficult body to replace. I continued to receive the highest annual appraisals and even "on the spot cash awards" (for saves). I had fit, by then, into the overall pattern of friction between management and controllers. And San Juan was not an easy facility to staff.

So how would we escape the clutches of chaos in Puerto Rico? Well, there is another facility that is even more difficult for the FAA to staff due to its complexities (and culture, I suppose): the New York Air Route Traffic Control Center, called ZNY, or New York Center, officially the NYARTCC. If ZNY wants something, they get it. I applied. They wanted me, and management in San Juan couldn't do anything about it, because ZNY was calling. Neither Susan nor I knew at the time that I had jumped out of the clutches of chaos and into the jaws of terror.

DRIFTING INTO THE WILD BLUE YONDER

After six years in Puerto Rico, we received an official promotion within the FAA that included a pay raise with a fully paid move. This meant assistance selling our home at a good price in Puerto Rico, a moving company packing up all our stuff and transporting it, keeping it stored for us in New York, an extended-stay hotel in New York, and assistance to purchase a home out on the east end of Long Island.

America, and New York in particular, immediately became healing balm to our tired and torn souls. The finest sushi, plush stores filled with all that we had missed, order on the highways, and people who spoke our language. Even the mostly uptight, always in a hurry, often-cold and sometimes hostile New York population was like soothing polish to us compared to all of the abrasive attitudes and grinding conditions we had just barely escaped over the last six years. We were so happy to be in New York! We were so glad to be home in the USA.

We spent several months in an extended-stay hotel on the taxpayer's dime while finally settling upon a lovely home in Shoreham, NY. It was the American dream. Susan was sitting pretty as she meticulously and artfully beautified the interior of our Long Island home in the loveliest of ways. We employed a landscaping service to care for the half-acre property, allowing us to enjoy a perfectly green, weed-free, wide-open and large manicured lawn. The yard was dressed with masses of purple rhododendrons and varying shades of pink azaleas. Large grey, arm-length sized stones that fit together to create a formidable and imposing wall adorned nearly 100 percent of the face of the home. This was out of the ordinary as far as what most suburban homes looked like from the street, but it helped us to feel sheltered, living behind that strong stone wall. It produced a powerful sense of privacy and tranquility. The only part of the home's front that wasn't stone was its entrance. An iron gate in the middle of the home's stone face opened into an open-sky atrium with footstones and a flower garden, and just beyond stood the secluded front door. On the flip side, one-third of the rear wall of the home was glass, from floor to high-vaulted ceiling, through which we viewed the landscaped backyard. We also enjoyed a large wrap-around fireplace in the living room, created out of the same two- to four-foot grey stones used on the front of the home. Susan painted green ivy borders all around the walls, where they met the ceiling, with various oil-painted (by hand) colorful flowers flowing throughout the ivy.

Susan became pregnant, twice. We purchased an RV and, between her pregnancies, began using it for winery tours with friends on the east end of Long Island, enjoying the Hamptons, and taking the family members who came to visit on tours. We also visited Niagara Falls in the RV and took some longer excursions here and there, from visiting family in Louisiana and Florida to eventually taking the children to the Sesame Street, Hershey's Chocolate Factory, and Crayola theme parks.

Admittedly, being in America propelled me into a bit of social imbalance, especially for New York. I don't know how to say it except—we were so happy! Many of our fellow New Yorkers had a different opinion. "This place sucks. Life sucks. What's the matter with you?" We tried to explain, "You should be grateful to live in America!"

There were a few happy and tender New Yorkers whom we met, and maintain relationships with still today, but the vast majority were in their own little country within this country, a culture to their own. But we didn't allow the sour attitudes of others to impact our celebratory, restorative mindset one iota. We were just so glad to be in the good ol' USA, living large and free.

Oh the smells of New York City! There were always various luring aromas of different ethnic foods in the air. We also frequented the city for dinners on special occasions and Broadway shows. We visited "Windows on the World" frequently, high atop the World Trade Center, a restaurant with amazing views on top of the Twin Towers. We took our family there when they came to visit us, or when we spent the day in Manhattan just for fun. We'd entered a season of great fulfillment and joy in New York. Susan took a management job at a Sears, and I sent her flowers at work regularly. We very much enjoyed the New York City culture (Broadway and more).

And now I knew I had made it. There was nowhere else I could go on earth to make more money or deserve more esteem in the use of my specific skill set. I had barely graduated high school, and now I was at the top of the world. In my mind, I had reached the absolute pinnacle of ATC, even being promoted to ZNY, where I would now enjoy the best equipment and top priority handling of any facility in America. It was such a contrast to the old, dilapidated equipment and armpit treatment of Puerto Rico with the "Now you're a real diva to be put on display" treatment of New York. All sorts of VIPs, from Congress-people to TV personalities, would come to tour the latest and greatest within our facility.

It is not a stretch to say that we New York Center controllers worked the most complex, condensed, and congested airspace sectors on the planet. I suppose controllers in Chicago or Los Angeles might argue that point, but New York has the dreaded, narrow NE corridor to manage with multiple points of departure and arrival within it. All that high-speed flight crammed into a condensed amount of terribly manipulated airspace sectors leaves no room for error, ever. You have to run them tight all day, every day, without wasting an inch.

Our specific dominion entailed part of the geographical NE corridor of the United States and most of the North Atlantic Ocean, reaching from just north of Puerto Rico toward Santa Maria (Spain), Shanwick (United Kingdom) and all the way around to Gander and Moncton (both, Canada)—3.27 million square miles of airspace to be exact. If you were to depart Miami and fly due east, you would eventually enter

New York's airspace. In the world of Air Traffic Control, ZNY is the large, snarling, slobbering silverback gorilla that's jumping up and down, pounding its fists on the floor, the biggest, "baddest" of them all.

Again, admittedly overjoyed, I joined the fold of controllers in ZNY and, once again, my abilities made room for me within the ATC environment, a harsh environment that I would eventually conform to. Initially, however, no matter the offensive attitude of gladness that incessantly exuded from me, my work performance overshadowed any opposition, to a vast extent, and I quickly progressed through the various ATC sectors, becoming a certified FPL in an uncharacteristic amount of time. It's not unreasonable for a transferring FPL to take five years or more to certify at ZNY. A brand new controller, starting from the bottom and working to FPL status, could take seven to nine years, or even more. That is, if the newbie made it at all. Many washed out altogether, FPL and newbie alike. I finished training, attaining the coveted FPL status, in a nearly unheard of two years and some change by January 1999.

Nationally, I qualified for a small group of air traffic controllers when I certified on New York's feared, vast oceanic airspace. Most controllers avoid such sectors like the plague, because the oceanic sectors are all non-radar: It's you with a mental picture, a pencil, a huge number of flight strips as your only visual reference, a clock, and a relaying station to issue your ATC commands for you. No microphone to simply key up and speak a command directly and instantly to a pilot, gaining his needed instant feedback. This weeds out a great number of controllers. If not their lack of desire or because of intimidation, then their lack of ability prohibited them from even approaching these sectors. All but the most skilled and driven need not apply.

The non-radar, oceanic work environment adds to the complexity of the job, and that's little-to-nothing like working air traffic in a tower at an airport or at a radarscope, as the overwhelming majority of air traffic controllers do in our country. I was assigned to Area E ("Area" is the official name for a group of ATC sectors) and it included one of New York's notoriously difficult radar sectors too—MANTA. Some seasoned FPL controllers would manipulate their days, all day long, to avoid working this man-eating radar sector, preferring even the unpopular non-radar sectors over it. Although I was told repeatedly it was a real bronco, I could stand, watch, and listen to what was going on and get the picture. At first, I was a little intimidated by MANTA, so complex with sick tunnels, corridors, and splintered corners and niches and edges and shelves of airspace. But I wasn't intimidated much, or for long, because I had never met a sector that I couldn't lasso, reel-in and control. My attitude was like, "Put me in coach! Let me at it!" They gave me a hardened trainer, the well-known, grumpiest, and one of the most respected controllers in the area. I find it interesting that being mean and being skilled were somehow related throughout my ATC career.

As I sat at the radarscope MANTA, JFK airport was on my scope, as was LaGuardia, Teterboro, Newark, Atlantic City, Philadelphia, Hartford, Providence, Boston and more. I say that to emphasize the reality that not all air traffic controllers are sitting in a tower at the airport. The more than twenty ARTCC's (Centers) in the continental US were built in the late 50s or early 60s, far from all areas of concentrated population. This was a strategy employed to maintain ATC in the event of a nuclear strike. I physically sat in Islip, NY, more than an hour's drive from Manhattan, but on the radarscope, which depicted hundreds of miles, I was only a few inches, quickly traversed on screen, from New York City.

Controllers who sit at the airport in ATC towers receive the lowest pay, and direct their aircraft to and from approach and departure controllers who sit at "approach control" (as it is called). Approach control is often located near the airport, maybe even stuffed into the tower on a lower floor, and these controllers receive medium pay within the overall ATC system. Finally, you have "center" controllers (ARTCC), which is where I worked. This is the highest pay-grade and involves en route traffic. The word en route may suggest level, already pointed in the right direction flights, but there's a whole lot of bobbing and weaving, climbing and descending to do in the en route environment. I worked flights departing from and destined to New York Center's airspace, to feed them and receive them to/from surrounding sectors (and, thereby, all over the world), in an orderly way to/from these airports, as well as others. I did both at the same time, taking and giving, without letting anyone smack another. There was a steady stream of departing and arriving flights, with crossing flights ascending and descending with heightened periods of traffic called rushes. The radar airspace was much smaller than I was used to in San Juan, and the speeds were routinely just the same. Fast. I was even there when the Concord was still flying and worked that aircraft many times. Imagine how fast the words from your lips go to reach the ear of the person next to you. The Concord flew faster than your words travelled to a nearby listener's ear. That is, faster than the speed of sound. I also worked Air Force One, the Pope's flight, and the private jets of movie stars, rock stars and so on.

I certified without any hiccups and fit right into the mix of rough and tumble New York air traffic controllers. Within about a year of becoming an FPL, I took on the overall attitude of the workers there. We were one filthy-mouthed, hard-hearted, and antagonizing group of people. Kick 'em while they're down and spit on 'em, and that sort of brutal, egotistic and domineering behavior.

It wasn't long before my chase for thrill found itself unsatisfied again. Now that I had everything in life that I had been gunning for, partying once again entered the scene. Looking back, I just couldn't get enough rush to be satisfied. I had such an attitude of being the law while plugged into ATC sectors—and that was appropriate—that this transferred to a real and inappropriate, "I am the law!" persona in every area of my life. I was the law, and I was going to do what I wanted to do when and how I wanted to do it. Being a FPL at New York Center wasn't enough. I lived recklessly, like spending several hundred dollars on a meal with friends (actually, in rivalry, we'd fight over the high tabs) a couple of times per week, and I had to have more. After a tough shift, a few strong hits of Jack Daniels helped carry me along in a sense of living a carefree, fast life. It became a habit, a way of supposed exhilaration.

My extracurricular activities never seemed to affect me

at work. I seemed to always receive kudos on the job and I did receive good official evaluations too. Everything in the work environment is recorded. Part of our evaluations included management randomly pulling the tapes without our knowledge for examination, some specifically for what we sounded like on the ATC frequencies and others for what we sounded like on frequencies and landlines combined. This was done periodically, two or three times per year, and the contents of the tapes were measured against the ATC manual for correctness and accuracy. We were required to speak by the book in the most intense situations no matter the emergency, kind of a tough mix, with being a human. These evaluations pulled more weight than behavior did, so when dudes were acting out or misbehaving, there was much leeway granted as long as their randomly pulled tapes sounded good. That's what mattered, even if, like me, the controller came to work looking like he hadn't had any sleep in four days from partying too much. All of this was my literal case. I've saved a randomly pulled, ATC frequency-only tape of me working, available on our YouTube channel http://bit.ly/2aBlEJf. It's from 2000 or 2001 in New York, while I was living wild. Everything is spoken meticulously by the book, as if reading from it during a not-so-busy session, although there was much more going on than what comes across on this tape, which doesn't include the landline coordination. This tape was a spot phraseology check, and I nailed it every time.

At home, more conflict surfaced between Susan and me. I think she wanted me to be a normal fella. Come home from work and start the barbecue, relax and chill. I think she wanted me to be a pillar and not need the alcohol or drugs to be happy. The intensity of the job was a superior reason (excuse) to abuse, and I played it for all it was worth. I think she wanted me to be fine, and the more I wasn't fine, the more she protested that I wasn't fine, and the more she unintentionally pushed me away from her. We began having quite a bit of frustration with one another. The children were mostly shielded from our marital discontentment. From the outside, we must have looked like a fairytale-come-true family.

Susan wanted to help me, I think, but her heart was broken and grew harder too. I was largely absent, physically and emotionally. It seemed there was nothing she could do for me. And vice-versa. Instead, we became captivated by one another's shortcomings. All I could see were her faults. All she could see were mine. We were living like that, just trudging through life, thinking that's just the way it was going to be.

Somewhere along the way a girl I knew from high school and I connected on the internet. It seemed like some things that I thought Susan wasn't giving me, whether she really was or not, were right there, available through this other woman who was eager and willing to give me what felt right. After some time on the internet we began meeting in Jacksonville, Florida, where she still lived. I flew anywhere for free. I'd just go through each checkpoint at the airport showing my FAA ID and usually be ushered right into the flight deck (cockpit) for a flight from New York to Florida. This wasn't an FAA approved procedure, but it worked. We controllers called it a "flash and dash." We were supposed to fill out official paperwork for each flight, but that took time, and they would keep track of where you were going. At the time, according to the official records, the most travelled-to destination by air traffic controllers in America was Las Vegas. I was but a thread in a much larger fabric of ATC stress-induced behavior.

I'd sit in the jump seat, which is an extra seat on the flight deck immediately behind the captain, or sometimes the airline would offer me a seat in first class. That was nice. I was carrying on that way and drinking, just being wild, and, really, very stupid. The other woman offered something that seemed to hit a certain spot in my heart, drawing me deeper into the muck. Of course, I didn't see it that way at the time. I thought my own desires were the law. I told Susan my many travels were work related and she believed me. So on and on I went, fast and feverishly chasing any and every thrill that I thought worthy of my pursuit.

Then my gears started to shift one January evening as I was leaving ZNY, going down the cement stairs after work. I slipped on some ice. It was just like a cartoon. My feet shot out from under me and, as I was falling uncontrollably, I could see that they were higher than my head. BAM! I landed squarely on my lower back. I laid there in agony for many minutes before peeling myself off of the ground and going back inside to fill out an on-the-job injury report. I'm sure I could've received some sort of disability retirement if I had pursued it. I did not. I was more interested in new access to unlimited pain pills.

So now there were alcohol, pain pills, occasional cocaine and weed, another woman, and loads of money bleeding away. I was earning about $150,000 a year at this point. And I myself was drifting away into the wild blue yonder. Any day that I went to work, if I wasn't in the mood or felt I had some other priority, I would just report to my supervisor that I had to take a pain pill for my back-related on-the-job injury. They would assign me non-safety related duties and I would breeze through the shift, getting off of work just in time to…get myself off. Without my knowing it, that whole "I am the law" thing was being flipped upside down in my life as I grew totally out of control. What a cycle and way of life. I was supposedly being satisfied by all the things I could have and all the things I wasn't allowed to have but enjoyed anyway. But, really, if I were indeed being satisfied with any of it, why would I continually reach for more and more and more? What was I chasing?

By September 2001, I was filing bankruptcy paperwork because my finances were so out of control. I sat in my attorney's office, looking out of his window as we discussed how I could smoothly skate by my obligations with the least amount of discomfort. Yes, that was the plan. I was in this man's office to deliberately see how I could escape the financial commitments I had gotten myself into, for the purpose of carrying on a truly unholy lifestyle. A lifestyle in which its major parts were clearly revealing the inner character of an adulterer. Now I know that one's character must be prepared, in advance, to successfully endure the storms of life. Sadly, back then, I was the storm. For example, the other woman divorced her husband for me. They had two children. I've deeply regretted that.

I wasn't being faithful to my wife, or the flying public

whom I once so zealously served and defended, or my employer who was paying me more than $12,000 per month. As I recall, my bankruptcy paperwork was officially filed on September 10, 2001.

THE DAY THE WORLD CHANGED

On September 11, 2001, I arrived at work, it so happened, sober and ready for duty at about 6:15 a.m. It was my sixth consecutive day of work, a day on overtime, supposedly a normal 6:30 a.m. to 2:30 p.m. shift. After sunrise the weather was dreamy clear blue skies, drastically reducing the complexities of my job. I was one of about ninety controllers on duty at New York Center that morning. Likewise, Boston Center had a similar number of controllers on duty that day, and Washington Center too, along with the other ARTCC's, a total of twenty-two within the contiguous states in America.

The shift began like normal. We would work a sector for about half an hour and then take a coffee break for twenty to forty minutes, rotating through the various air traffic control sections of airspace within our area. After rotating through a few sectors of airspace that morning, I was working an oceanic, non-radar sector just off of the coast of Long Island. The sector I was working always included an assigned assistant who sat directly next to the controller as a set of proofreading eyes and also to answer various landlines for the primary controller of that airspace (sector). My assistant that morning was a newbie, still aspiring to become an FPL. She sat directly next to me in front of new technology that was a computer-generated, not-for-control-decisions display of my airspace and its traffic. This screen displayed the airspace over Manhattan.

Things were moving along as normal when I heard "Giant Killer" call over a landline loud speaker (or "shout line"). Unlike when you answer the phone at home, having to take action to hear what the caller has to say, in the ATC environment the atmosphere is filled with shouting controllers broadcasting a wide variety of requests or information into the control room. Giant Killer is a USAF air defense facility that guards our nation's skies for national security. They have the power and authority to launch United States attack jets toward any perceived aviation threat for its destruction. ATC did not target planes for annihilation, but we routinely worked with Giant Killer hand in hand.

The newbie assigned to me picked up a handset to specifically answer Giant Killer's shout and, upon listening to their question via the handset, did not know how to answer. She turned to me and said, "Giant Killer is asking if we can confirm there is a hijacked aircraft flying over Manhattan."

I leaned over to the computer-generated screen and noted, among all the other air traffic depicted, an aircraft that was a primary target only, meaning the aircraft's transponder was off, whether intentionally or unintentionally, and not relaying critical flight data to ATC. I pointed that target out to her and then instructed her to relay to Giant Killer that we had a primary target (official phrase for said situation) over Manhattan, but could not confirm it was a hijacking. At this point, Giant Killer had numerous military air traffic controllers who specialize in national defense on numerous landlines with numerous FAA air traffic controllers, gathering information to assess what was going on and how to respond.

The newbie complied with my instructions, and we both went back to our normal duties. Within minutes Giant Killer called back and I could hear the urgency in the voice on the shout line, "New York, can you confirm that the primary target has now hit the World Trade Center?" My assistant snatched up the handset to communicate a message back to Giant Killer while simultaneously giving me a perplexed look which clearly prompted me for an answer. I quickly noted that the primary target had vanished in the vicinity of Manhattan. Buildings were not displayed on the screen, only airways and intersections in the sky. Knowing that whatever I said next would be heard through her handset, I barked, "I don't know! Why don't you watch CNN!" In my arrogance I meant to be rude toward the Giant Killer controller, having no idea that the very words I spoke would become an international event. This comment haunted me for years, being so proud and insensitive toward the gravities of my job.

Of course, now everybody knows that's exactly how the world learned of the attack. Mind you, there were no TVs in our control room, and I would have never imagined that an aircraft would intentionally fly into the Twin Towers. Within minutes the entire world, as well as Giant Killer, I suppose, was watching CNN to see endless reruns of a hijacked aircraft deliberately flying into the World Trade Center. At this point, we were likely among the few who understood that it was a hijacked aircraft and not just a terrible accident. Within moments of the first impact, chatter between controllers in different centers swept throughout each facility.

My turn came up for a break. I rushed to the cafeteria where there was a TV to see what everyone in the facility was now talking about, a jet that had impacted one of the two Twin Towers. Things unfolded so fast.

After watching CNN for about twenty minutes I returned to my area to work air traffic again, pumped up on adrenaline by what I had just seen. As I walked down the hallway between the cafeteria and control room, I muttered to myself, "America is under attack." There was a buzz of near unbelief and dismay throughout the facility. I plugged heart and soul into MANTA, the radar sector which allowed me to see and work live air traffic with a specific eye upon the airspace over Manhattan. The sector was running with a busy flow of air traffic when the second impact to the Twin Towers took place, with seemingly everyone from the military to the FAA now watching.

Within moments, all of the nation's air traffic controllers were directed by management to halt the flow of air traffic by commanding every flight to land immediately. We had to scramble to find appropriate runways for every single flight. Now no flight was permitted to continue to its originally stated, intended destination unless, of course, they were all but there. This caused a huge challenge, because if a controller tried to set a jet down on a runway that was too short for it to land on, more disasters would undoubtedly unfold. Larger jets require longer runways, all the more if still loaded with fuel. In fact, many had to dump thousands of gallons of jet fuel just to land at all, not to mention the havoc this caused to the overall flow of traffic that was in the sky.

The war was in full swing and the morning was still so young. Giant Killer launched USAF attack jets (F-15s and F-16s), coordinating with us, to perform Combat Air Patrol (CAP) over Manhattan through my specific sector. Many other cities in America also had US attack jets overhead, just in case. I worked the CAP flights to and from Manhattan, while plugged into MANTA.

We had a mix of armed and ready US attack jets along with civilian airliners and private aircraft in our skies, and we were working feverishly, like never before, to interrogate every single instance of perceived resistance to our commands. If a pilot so much as stuttered, it crossed my mind that he too may be a hijacker.

A jet struck the Pentagon. News spread throughout the facility that America had at least two dozen confirmed hijacked flights in her airspace, news we would only much later learn wasn't true. "SCATANA" crossed my mind from way back in 1987 military ATC school. It stands for Security Control of Air Traffic and Air Navigational Aids. This was a government plan formulated in the 1960s so if the Soviet Union tried to invade America we could shut down every ground based air-navigation aide to hinder the Soviet effort, and ground all of our aircraft too. Sounds great now, in light of 9/11, but SCATANA was something we mulled over in school for about a half hour and then we moved on to other training for potential emergency scenarios. To this day, I've not heard a single other air traffic controller who was on duty in America on 9/11 bring up SCATANA. But that's exactly what was on my mind and what we were all doing, altogether shutting down America's skies.

The US attack jets aggressively investigated anything we reported to them that didn't smell right. One private pilot somehow got off the ground at Republic Airport in Farmingville, NY. Apparently he thought he'd do some sightseeing, some disaster rubbernecking around Manhattan. About halfway from Farmingville to New York City, a couple of F-16s on CAP were dispatched to greet him. They purposely flew at a high rate of speed toward the small aircraft, just barely missing the aviator's cockpit, causing him to scream over the air traffic control emergency frequencies, "MAYDAY! MAYDAY! MAYDAY! I'm turning back! Okay, okay! I'm turning back! Please! I'm turning back. Returning to Farmingville right now!"

I was also plugged-in and working when United 93 was downed in Pennsylvania. I saw plenty of far out stuff on the scopes that day and was intimately involved in providing air traffic control for America on its undisputedly most horrific aviation day in history. Meanwhile, it occurred to me that the same air-conditioned, dark and comfy building where I sat would be a superior target for the terrorists. To take out any center, I thought while working feverishly, would instantly leave the flying public in a state of hopeless chaos.

By now, word had spread throughout the control room that a FedEx truck had come and unloaded a S.W.A.T. team to protect us from harm. I thought, *Really, they can stop a 747 from crashing into us?* I knew they could not, and was afraid for my own life. In the past, it was everyone else who was at risk of dying, and no matter what, I would be just fine.

As I sat in front of the radarscope that day, it was the first time in my arrogant controller career that the smug sense of safety, stemming from the philosophy of "Well, if you die I will still be okay," was removed.

I was so stricken with terror as I sat at MANTA that I irrationally kept an eye on the airspace directly over my home where I knew my wife and children were. Surely no terrorist was going to single out a suburban home, far removed from any tactical significance, to destroy it. But these were the kinds of things that my sober, racing mind considered in the fog of homeland war that day; that is, those of us who were "in control." Truthfully, no one in America was really in control.

Nevertheless, we kept pushing tin until all of the domestic flights were safely on the ground, even as I continued to rotate through my area's air traffic control sectors. It is truly miraculous, from this former air traffic controller's perspective, that there were not more aviation disasters that day. There could have very easily been mid-air collisions or runway incursions. In fact, it's still hard for me to wrap my head around the fact that those types of other aviation disasters did not take place either as a result of the attack or our required duty of grounding the entire aviation industry in such a short amount of time. Odds are, more disasters should have happened.

At about 1:00 p.m. management asked for volunteers to stay beyond their normal shift's end. While by then all of the domestic flights were safely on the ground, we still had many commercial airliners that were inbound to America, crossing the Atlantic Ocean. They were too far along to turn back. It remained to be seen how many of them might have hostile intentions toward the homeland.

That traffic had to be worked too, flight by flight. I volunteered to stay for overtime and remained on duty even after my normal overtime shift ended. We painstakingly diverted all of the transatlantic flights either to Canada or the Caribbean, according to their ability, and refused to receive a single airliner on our home turf.

Going home from ZNY on 9/11 felt eerie and strangely familiar. Long Island had been locked down by the government. Nobody could get on or off what we were now being reminded was an island. On this horrific day we found ourselves helplessly bound to whatever was going to happen, like all those years in Puerto Rico. It was amazing that they could do that. We had no idea!

When I finally reached home, I found that Susan had asked her 15-year-old niece, who was living with us at the time, to watch our children so we could escape to a local tavern and try to unwind together. I was shaken to the core, to an extent that Susan had never seen in me before. She wanted to help but there was really nothing she could do.

Early the next morning, I sprung straight up out of bed from a vivid nightmare. The dream was so real that when I shot up with a gasp of life-saving air it felt as though my life had just been saved. I was dying under the weight of the rubble of the Twin Towers in this lucid vision.

September 12, 2001, marked the beginning of nightly escapes from the Grim Reaper's vicious, incarnate teeth, by the hair on my chin, numerous times per week. I just can't say with enough clarity or emphasis how very real these dreams were. I was having actual near-death experiences several times a week. And I tasted every kind of death imaginable too. I can't imagine any form of death that I did not personally and intimately experience—car crashes, cannibalism, plane crashes, cliff falls, Dracula, and so on. Susan said my nighttime body tics included flailing arms and legs, so that she stopped sleeping in the same bedroom with me.

The day after the terrorist attack on the Twin Towers was what the government considered my "regular day off." I got bombed. Just like the Twin Towers, my life had begun to come crashing down, and it wouldn't be long before we, too, were but a heap of ruins.

Susan was terrified because for a while we couldn't get off of the island. New York was the last place you wanted to be, but we couldn't leave. Missiles might be coming, and we couldn't evacuate. As the days and weeks went by, she feared that the drinking water would be poisoned. When the Anthrax scare hit in New Jersey, she would get our mail out of the mailbox wearing rubber gloves and a mask, and not bring it into the house for a period of time. I learned that some of the 9/11 hijackers had used the "flash and dash" method, as I had done so many times. They dressed up as professional pilots to take advantage of what was a widely practiced courtesy to aviators at the time, free entrance to the cockpits of the flights they later took control of to destroy. They flashed their fake IDs and were ushered onto the flight deck for unobstructed access–to the pilots and the planes.

America's ATC system went wheels-up, launching back into full swing on September 13th, my first day back to work after my regular day off on the 12th. I asked management for a stress related on-the-job injury report to file because I was still very shaken. The official procedure for a controller in my state would be to fill out that form and go see a shrink. I had done that a few times over my career after especially close calls or other dramatic events. One time before 9/11 someone–a terrorist I suppose–flooded the New York ATC control room with weed-killer fumes through the facility's air intake system, filling the entire workspace with noxious chemicals.

If it was warranted, the doctor could order a traumatized controller to stay home from work with full pay to recuperate for from a day to six weeks. As I filled out the report on September 13, 2001, a union representative, a local and a controller who was not there on 9/11, approached me and said, "If you turn in that form I am going to kick your ass in the parking lot. America's hurting right now and you can't do that." I thought, *I am America!* But by then, I was certainly an expert at separating everything from physical pain to troubled feelings from myself for the purpose of working air traffic. I went straight back to pushing tin that day, the 13th of September, 2001.

I did file the form, but it obviously vanished. Nothing ever came of it and my recent inquiry for the official records makes it look as though the form was never filed. I did officially try to get help, and found none. I self-medicated.

That night slapped me with another vivid nightmare in which I just barely escaped the tearing teeth of living-death. Another normal shift at work, then some booze. More nightmares. I began drinking more alcohol and using more drugs, trying to shield myself or insulate myself from the dreadful pain and literal terror: death, death, death. Every form of living through death, daily.

The dreams were so frequent and real that I couldn't shake them off. In the daytime, I could do my job, but when I got off of work I was deeply bothered no matter what I tried. I couldn't shake death off of me. The dreams were so profound that they began changing my daytime behavior. I had become like a machine, working air traffic without any regard for my human, emotional needs, or any consideration of my own physical needs either (restful sleep, back-pain relief, etc.). Since the attack on America, this task-oriented machine was working like a war-battered armored military vehicle, at the cost of being a person. I was a master at insulating myself from pain for the day, but totally inadequate to gain relief from my nighttime demons.

It would take an act of God to reset me after 9/11.

FLAMEOUT

We followed through with the bankruptcy proceedings, which excused about $60,000 worth of unsecured debt. The debt was just swept away. That was one case where paying a New York attorney worked to our advantage, although I'm sure it didn't seem as favorable to those who were left holding the bag. The only adverse impact we felt was in carrying a bankruptcy on our credit record for about a decade. We learned our lesson and entered a long season of carrying no debt whatsoever, except the mortgage debt on our dream home.

In January 2002, four agonizing months after 9/11, I got a surprise call at home one evening from the FAA flight surgeon, "Robert, we've got a problem with the recent drug test you've submitted." I don't recall exactly how I responded to him, other than to deny any wrongdoing. This phone call was a penetrating terror to my wife. I felt tremendous compassion for her. My job was her tower of security, and this call was like another of the World Trade Center buildings that was crashing down, and now, in our living room. I was already in a desperate, crumbling state, and now our only source of income began to come crashing down as well.

"Failure to comply with drug testing procedures" was the official charge, stemming from the appearance that the sample had been adulterated, and that's a biggie. Everyone in the agency knew that to be charged with said offense meant you were through dealing; your days were finished. Of course, I hired a $300 per hour New York attorney who assured me that he could beat the charge for me, whether I was guilty or not. The FAA pulled me off of the control room floor and placed me at a desk until everything could get sorted out.

Only while fighting the government in court much later did I learn that the official course of action for that specific offense calls for the chief of ZNY to "initiate the removal process from employment." That's different than "remove from employment," which was my understanding at the time. He was only required to begin the firing process. He wasn't required to all-out fire me no matter what. For years I had heard that it's impossible to get fired from the US government. My confidence was in that notion and my attorney, so I funneled tens of thousands of dollars to him. If I would have understood that the chief had some leeway, I may have gone to him while he was initiating the removal process and asked to be sent to rehab. He likely would have granted that, having fulfilled the initial step of the required procedures, and excused my offense. I mean, after all my career record was absolutely clean, and I had only good official evaluations, not to mention I was a 9/11 vet. Looking back, rehab would have been good for me. However, my brilliant New York attorney–whose instructions I followed, I wasn't paying him for nothing–also only learned of the aforementioned nuance while we were in court. Misplaced confidence—pride—was my downfall.

The truth is, I did tamper with the drug test. There are all sorts of products advertised on the internet designed to help someone evade detection if their sample is "hot." Caution to all loose cannons out there: they don't always work. Though guilty, I perceived the agency to be utterly inept at doing just about anything right, so I placed my confidence in the hope that they had screwed up the process of gathering my sample, or that my attorney could find some other evidence which would invalidate the sample altogether.

Looking back, I wish I would have never been so wild—to use alcohol the way I did, or drugs, or women, or been so arrogant either. I wish I had been more insistent to get professional help in the days after 9/11. But I was angry and arrogant, somehow considering the government as my opponent rather than a place to serve. I firmly believed they didn't care about me or the public; all they wanted, I had concluded, was for things to move along smoothly and quietly. If I weren't so mad about that, I may have found the wherewithal to ask for help again, like I did on 9/13. It's so sad to me that doing the best I could worked out the way it did.

While assigned to a desk, I continued running around like a wild man, cheating on Susan by flying to Florida to see the other woman, drinking, taking pain pills, having nightmares, and repeating this cycle over and over and over again. In February 2002, my stepbrother Michael died at 35 years old from complications of a car crash. I was so wrapped up in my own downward spiral that I didn't even attend his funeral. I was indeed out of control.

After one unbridled tangent weekend in Florida, Susan came to the airport to greet me upon my return to New York. While I drove us home via the freeway, we held hands and prayed The Lord's Prayer. Hurting as we both were, and me fresh off of an adulterous weekend, the prayer was heartfelt for me. I noticed a beautiful harmony in our voices together as we prayed. I don't know how it sounded to God, but it was remarkable and special to me. The moment we said Amen a school-bus-sized snowplow made a 90-degree turn off of the middle median and into our lane directly in front of us. I jammed on the brakes and did the best I could to avoid a horrid crash, missing the giant piece of moving steel by a hair. Did the prayer prompt the incident? As in, "I hear you, and you are headed for serious trouble!" Or did the prayer provide our way of escape? Both, I believe. At the time, we did see it as a sign, understanding that we were in big trouble, but not really knowing what to do about it. We knew to pray, but did not know what to do after praying.

In March 2002, my stepfather, Jim, died from a brief, losing bout with cancer. I moved Susan and the children down to Florida to help my mother. The other woman ended up posing as a family friend, and we conspired to have her watch the children while Susan and I attended Jim's memorial service. Later, the other woman manipulated Susan. She would take her shopping, call her to chat, and generally felt out how she was doing or how she felt about our marriage. Little did Susan know at the time that the other woman had an ulterior motive.

After the memorial service, a line of friends and relatives

passed in front of our bereaved family to offer condolences. An aunt whom I hadn't seen since I was a kid worked her way through the row of immediate family members to shake each hand, and when she arrived in front of Susan who was standing in line beside me, my aunt busted out in a different language, what some Christians call "tongues." She was yammering and yapping out loud, with tears, holding Susan's hand and not letting it go. It was bizarre and senseless babbling to us. She seemed like such a weirdo. Susan and I just stood there, glancing at one another in perplexity. The aunt didn't do that with anyone else at the memorial service.

When she stopped rambling on like a lunatic, Aunt Annette began speaking English to Susan and me, still holding Susan's hand and now grabbing mine, "Jesus has set you two apart, and there's a great call of God on your lives. So much glory is come to you, shall rest upon you, and overtake many, many others through your lives."

We nodded and politely replied, "Thank you."

After the service we spoke to one another about how peculiar and cracked she was. Neither of us put any weight on what she said, or thought anything of the event until years later. We would eventually become fully convinced that she was the one who was spot on and we were the senseless lunatics.

Back in New York, it was just me, our barren home since Susan and the kids stayed behind to help my mother, and my desk job, along with the living-death which was wrenching me day and night. I did go to a bar on lunch break one time with a co-worker friend. As we sat there drinking, I said to him, "Do you think God is trying to tell me something? I mean, I'm being charged with adulterating a urine sample while I'm committing adultery."

My friend, who had a tattoo of the devil, replied, "Na -man! Are you kidding? You're in the zone! You got it made. You have a sweet wife and a hot girlfriend, plus you're about to take the FAA to the bank!" I suppose he told me what I wanted to hear at the time, although I wasn't completely convinced he was right.

My Mondays through Fridays were horribly lonely and tormented, especially the evenings. During the days at my desk, I was all hopped-up on pain pills. I had no one to go to or be with in the evenings, not wanting to incriminate by association any of my co-workers. The lonely house was a gigantic loudspeaker that incessantly blared my doom and I couldn't avoid going there to abide. It was a time that prompted me to face myself and what I saw in the mirror was an unbearable sight. I considered what my actions were doing to my wife and innocent, flawless children, and how losing the job I had invested all of my energy, soul, joy and hopes into was all but imminent. I barely survived on the sliver of hope that my attorney would do as he promised.

Finally, in June 2002, I went to Florida for a loose weekend that would mark another forever change in our lives. I flew out of Islip, NY, that fateful Friday evening. I was still dressed to kill, looking so professional in an expensive suit, and quickly brandished my FAA ID for favors. I had already popped a few pain pills before going to the airport that evening. While I waited for the flight at the terminal, enjoying a pre-flight whiskey, a stranger came and sat down next to me and struck up a conversation. The following week I was to wonder if he was a private investigator for the FAA or for the ZNY chief personally who had been wondering what to do with me for nearly six months. That stranger asked some unusual questions, and at the time it didn't occur to me that my answers might actually matter. I spoke to him of having friends "in the company" (the mafia) in response to one of his questions, and I shared other tainted parts of my life with him as well. Then we both boarded the flight.

I took an aisle seat in coach and shortly thereafter ordered myself a drink. As I enjoyed my triple-Jack with a splash of Coke, I noticed a man in Muslim garb sitting in the window seat next to me. He ordered a can of Heineken but when the flight attendant gave it to him, he tucked it away without opening it. Then he took out a notebook and began sketching the different major landmarks, like bridges, that we could see as we flew over them.

This didn't sit right with me. I don't have anything, in general, against any religious groups. But fresh off of 9/11 and with Darvocet (pain killers) and whiskey fresh in my system, it looked to me like an enemy combatant was sitting right next to me gathering Intel.

Reeking of whiskey, I am sure, I got up and went to the front of the cabin to report my perceptions to the flight attendant, showing what I knew they often misunderstood to be an FAA inspector's badge (my government ID). I thought that would make her listen to me, despite my breath. I suppose Mr. Mystery-man with the peculiar questions was on board observing me, too. I continued to present myself as the FAA, and as exceptionally alarmed, to the flight attendant, insisting that she tell the captain I was reporting something wrong.

After a few minutes she returned to me, still standing in the aisle, and said not to worry about it. I did not initially comply. I continued to show my FAA ID and insist that something was very wrong, finally returning to my seat to just ride it out. We landed in Baltimore where I needed to change planes before continuing on to Florida. As everyone filed off of the aircraft I noted that the cockpit door was open. I stepped up and continued to insist, personally, to the captain that the other passenger may be up to no good.

He replied, "Call the FBI then."

I didn't. I deplaned and went to my next gate. There, I showed my badge again and told the whole disturbing perception to the attendant, who was not at all interested. In my buzzed state of mind, I dropped the issue and turned my focus to the fling awaiting me in Florida.

I don't know what happened to the accused Muslim artist, or the inquisitive stranger. If the stranger was indeed an investigator, he may have not even realized that I was torqued. I was a functioning addict, meaning that it would have been difficult for most people to detect that I was under the influence at all. I can understand that when someone hears about me taking a couple of pain pills and then downing near straight whiskey they would consider that I must have been really hammered. However, I used to drink two-thirds of a bottle of whiskey, along with a 12-pack of beer, on top of pain pills while using cocaine and pot. Daily. A functioning addict. Having said all that, I was buzzed on this flight, not a drunk fool, but fully convinced regarding the artist and motivated to speak up by the uninhibitedness that alcohol brings to the equation.

Anyway, that Friday night I continued on to Florida and did whatever I had been doing for quite some time, living loose, large and "free." Then I flew back to New York Sunday evening completely exhausted in every imaginable way. There was no intoxicate nor any extracurricular activity that could slow the vivid, constant close encounters with death through my nights. Death was alive and tormenting me. Furthermore, I was tired of living so many lies under the extreme stress of trying to keep it all together and going. I was tired of "running around" and manipulating everyone and everything to continue the same. I was simply and utterly spent.

I got back to my car at the Islip airport that Sunday night and just sat, exhausted, in the driver's seat with my car keys in my hand. My key ring had a piece of glass with an etched hologram of Jesus' face and head wearing the crown of thorns. Over the years it had been a sort of touch point for me to pray. I didn't see it as a good luck charm or believe it had any supernatural powers to bless me. It was just a reminder to me that Jesus loved me, even in my adulterous state.

So with my hand firmly clutching all of my keys, together with this key ring in my fist, I prayed, "Jesus. I can't do this anymore. Please God, help me. I just can't keep going on like this anymore." I sat quietly with a few tears streaming down my face and eventually began to place the key into the ignition. That's when I noticed Christ's holographic face and head had completely and entirely vanished from the etched glass. The glass was perfectly clear and empty, with nothing on it at all. We're talking etched glass that had suddenly lost its etching!

How on earth could that happen? I thought. *That's impossible.* I didn't realize the biblical significance at the time of "God hiding His face" from someone, but have since learned that it means one has lost God's favor, a terror in itself to the discerning. I drove home without Jesus' face on my key-chain that Sunday night, perplexed by its disappearing act.

I went to work at my desk Monday morning, back at ZNY for another week of the same old, same old. One of the managers, one that most of the controllers despised, came and got me at about 9:00 a.m. to take me to the chief's office. This was the first time I said anything to the chief whatsoever since the January removal from the control room floor. He had been wanting to meet with me, but I had followed my attorney's advice and avoided that, allowing my attorney to represent me.

That Monday morning, I was informed that I was no longer favored by the FAA, that I had been fired. A judgment had come to me from one who had the authority to terminate my career. Did the Friday evening interactions with Mr. Mystery-man get back to the chief? Did the airline from that night report a rogue air traffic controller, named Robert Totman, to the FAA? I was dumbfounded. I'd like to say "speechless" but, worse yet, I think I may have told them they were making a mistake they would surely regret, with Federal court in my mind. I was sure a judge would make them give me my job back, with back pay. Nevertheless, on my little sister's birthday, Monday, June 17, 2002, my FAA ID was taken away, my very identity with it, and I was escorted to my car where I was then instructed to leave the FAA facility.

DEATH SPIRAL

The beginning of 2002 brought such loss. First my stepbrother, then my stepfather. And I did the impossible by getting fired from my esteemed government career and lost my only identity with it. Then I had to begin the process of selling my American-dream suburban home, all within the first six months of that year. Yes, just like the Twin Towers, tall and stately as my life had been, built for all to esteem and admit as solid and good, now seemed destined to be a heap of smoldering ruins, brought down suddenly and with absolute finality.

I moved back to Florida defeated and ashamed, confused, scattered and yet still prideful. Inwardly, I was a total mess. Outwardly, even still, I clung to the sliver of hope that I could win a victory against the FAA in Federal Court. Frankly, the FAA did break the chain of custody while collecting my drug test urine sample. We had evidence. When a urine sample is collected for drug testing, it is important that the person who submits the sample is credited with whatever results come forth. There are a myriad of steps and safeguards to protect the integrity of the entire collecting process, however these important steps do get screwed up sometimes, and in my case they did. They botched my collection process, leaving paperwork evidence of the mistake. The technicality was quite plain and my New York attorney jumped on it. I had heard of controllers getting off for the same set of circumstances, but that wasn't the case for me. I don't know how or why I didn't, other than it was God's plan. To me, that makes what happened all the more mysterious, even mystical, like the etched glass losing its etching while I prayed. I wonder where I'd be if I had won in court. Dead, I bet. I cashed in the six-figure retirement I had built up over my fifteen-year career; it was, incredibly, untouched by our bankruptcy. With some humility, that surely could have supported my family for several years. But I continued living how I was accustomed to living, from trips to the beach in the RV to Ruth Chris Steakhouse as often as I desired, even upholding two separate "intimate" relationships with the women in my life. I was hurting deeply, had no solid identity and a nebulous, at best, view of my future. I felt self-hatred and self-torment for throwing away what I was only now beginning to properly appreciate—an esteemed career—and this was in addition to the endless, slim escapes from the vicious, living jaws of death numerous times per week through the always shocking and devastating nightmares.

I drank, a lot. I found myself absolutely hammered on multi-day drug and alcohol binges, to the point of not being able to stay awake at the wheel of my RV while driving my children around. I accidently ran red lights more than once in this state of oblivion. It certainly occurred to me that it would be safer and better for my children to not be around me, that in fact they would be much better off without me. There were still all sorts of comforts readily available to me, to help me feel better about my predicament. Susan was there and wanted to help. The other woman was there and wanted to help. Drugs and alcohol were there, insisting they could help. My beloved beach was there, the shiny RV was there, a somewhat fat bank account was there—all asserting their ability to help me. My children's sweet faces and innocent hearts broke my own crumbling heart all the more, as I realized they deserved so much more than what I could ever give them.

I thought an affair would be pleasant, having my cake and eating it too. I didn't see any reason whatsoever to restrain myself from satisfying what my eyes wanted. As I yielded to my desires and that season of my life matured, I found that instead of eating sweet cake I had been thrown into a den of starving lions like a piece of raw meat. I was being torn apart from the inside out. Here I had thought I was getting for myself life, life, life and more life, but all the while something mystical was working behind the scenes to bring me down, down, down to death, death, and more death. I was experiencing a multiplied effect of unbreakable truths and the fruit of the seeds I had been sowing was coming to bear, fully.

Now I began to look at Susan with great affection. The things that bothered me about her when we lived in New York together had been washed away by how she treated my widow mother and remained steadfast by my straying side—even though she had deep suspicions about my relationship with the other woman. She had noticed how the two of us interacted before my stepfather's memorial, when the other woman babysat our children, and she was pretty sure we were not like "brother and sister," as we insisted. She confronted me numerous times, but I always denied her accusations. To prove her commitment to me, she would do anything I asked of her. I knew that the only reasonable response to this type of devotion would be all-out faithfulness in return.

But the other woman offered me a whole different life, one with promises of satisfaction as well. It seemed that she too would do anything I asked of her, also requiring nothing less of me than my all-out faithfulness to her. Both women had two innocent and perfectly lovely children. I was the ugly in all of their individual and collective lives. Tearing jaws locked upon my flesh and were ripping me in two through these relationships all day, every day. At night my nightmares were also having their way with me, so that night and day echoed the same thing—torment.

I was angry, a lot. The thrust of the anger was pointed at myself, but also found its gaze upon the FAA and, sadly, at the women closest to me, even for the most insignificant of reasons. The anger was boiling over and spilling out on them. Faithfulness was not in me, except perhaps toward the children. I can honestly say that I never hit anyone physically, but I'm sure I loosed a tyrant of verbal self-hatred toward the women regularly, without actually physically attacking them as I boiled over. The rage was vented through drugs, alcohol and self-loathing, into routinely knocking myself out with these substances.

Again, there was no solution in sight. Federal court

proceedings unfolded against me. I was a drifter, living in my RV and bouncing back and forth between the two women and their homes, with stays at the beach in between.

By spring of the next year, something broke within me toward making up my mind to favor my family. I had wavered back and forth between the two women for years now, deciding to fully commit one way and then the other. I have to say that no degree of commitment to the other woman ever saw me fully surrender the idea of my family being fully intact. The spring of that year saw me abandon her for this idea that I could never wholeheartedly give up. I left the other woman's house for the last time. Susan was being torn by all of the conflict in our relationship too, but I don't think that was the case with the other woman. She was just a crazy-powerful magnet. Susan wanted me back, but our relationship was an absolute wreck. On the short drive from the other woman's home to my wife's apartment, I prayed, "God, You've got to do something. Susan and I have nothing left. Our marriage is dead. I'm returning to her, for my family, God, and asking You for a miracle. We have to have a miracle from You or this won't work."

I told no one about this, but obviously now had more time to begin spending with Susan and the children. I don't think that she had much love for me at this point, but I do think she had an undying devotion to the idea of having our family together. It seemed that was common ground for us. We both wanted a healthy, happy family. We moved from the apartment and bought a modest condominium in a duplex. Susan began regularly attending a nearby Episcopal Church with the children. They heard about me there and began praying for the former 9/11 New York air traffic controller who was a father in such bad shape.

For a few months after leaving the other woman, I attended church with my family a handful of times at most. I found no sudden relief through my choice, church attendance, prayer, or devotion to the family. Rather, I specifically recall lying on the couch in the living room one early morning, coming down off of a binger and feeling deep, deep despair. While I laid there under the weight of my utter devastation, thinking of how ruined I was (by this point, even the six-figure retirement funds that I had cashed in were exhausted), I saw a spiritual messenger of death like I had seen in my dreams many times before. But now I was not at all dreaming. I was most certainly awake, in my living room, watching this dark entity fly through the room and toward my face. I knew it was Death and it had come to take me away. I felt as though my time was short; I was not so much afraid as I was yielding to the idea of being completely finished with my time in the earth. I was ready to die, for everyone's benefit. As the entity continued to get closer and closer to my face it seemed to fade away. Did it fly into me? Or just vanish? I didn't know.

After that morning, I began planning how I would take my own life. A couple of weeks later, I had settled upon a shotgun blast to the head in the backyard. I told Susan of my misery and, without details, also told her that I was thinking about suicide. It had been more than two years of continual desolation. She didn't want to see me suffer anymore, whatever that meant. I'm not saying that she wanted me to die. But she began to have glimmers of hope for a better life and was ready to cut the weight of me loose, to breakup, if that's what it would take for me to be happy. She was ready for a divorce, believing there was nothing she could do for me. We filled out all of the necessary paperwork for a divorce and wrote the check for its ratification, placing the materials within a postage-paid envelope. Our divorce was literally signed, sealed, paid for and all but delivered.

But God had an entirely different kind of delivery in mind.

"GOOD DAY"*

In the past, we knew to pray, but did not know what to do after we prayed. When we were teenagers, Susan and I had both asked Jesus to be our Savior. But there's no doubt that neither of us had made any attempt whatsoever to live our day-to-day practicalities with Him. We were about to learn that God had been listening to our prayers all the while and agonizing through our sufferings right along with us; that all the while, He was right there and eager to help us out of our misery and into a different, extraordinary type of life.

A few days after I saw the angel of death in my living room, I went to visit the priest where Susan had been attending church. I was miserable and desperate and under a suicidal influence. I had concluded that everyone I knew would be better off without me around. The priest told me that my misery was the result of my own sinful choices. I did not have any more fight in me to argue the point. I got it, having no ground to stand upon and oppose him from. He was right.

* "Good Day" is an ATC salutation world-wide. It's not in the ATC manual, but we regularly used it to welcome pilots to our control upon initially establishing two-way communications. As in, "Good day–you are safe with me in control."

I had never heard it, however, in the way the priest said it. He informed me that I had been living in "idolatry" before God. I understood that idolatry meant openly opposing God. That term made it click in me, a specific thing I had been doing was obviously opposed to God. Before I first laid with the adulteress, I pondered aloud with her, "Do you think God will forgive us?" I was aware of God, but not concerned enough about living within His blessing or approval rather than this ludicrous position I had placed myself in. I thought myself "saved" all those years, but now realized that I had been living in idolatry–specifically, cherishing what I wanted more than what God wanted for me. The priest helped me by reading a prayer and having me repeat after him, if I agreed with his words. I repeated and meant everything he read. There was no massive awakening at that moment. But it had been done in faith, and I couldn't help but believe that I was getting off the hook with God regarding all my terrible actions. I "got" the gravity of idolatry and the gravity of Jesus' work. I mean, I believed it, just a little bit. I didn't know what to expect in coming days. But it felt good to come clean with God.

However, there was no sudden impact from that day, and I continued living in the misery I had brought upon myself. Although I had bared it all with God, asked for forgiveness, accepting the cross of Christ as His answer and pledged to live in a way that would be pleasing to Him, try as I might, I continued on the exact same course. After three or four weeks since meeting with the priest, I did not witness any change. In fact, I had traversed another two or three cocaine, pills, and whiskey binges. The guilt was too much. It was time to halt this pattern before my children were physically injured by my recklessness. That's when I made up my mind that I would indeed kill myself.

Veteran suicide is an all-too-frequent tragedy in our country. Medically, I had been suffering PTSD too, but PTSD was never even uttered to me (or about me, as far as I know) and I received zero professional treatment for it either. I bet a lot of desperate veterans feel this way: Those I love are suffering because of me. It's a reasonable sacrifice to take the source of pain—me—out of the equation. I'd made my decision and felt as though I needed to seal the deal with God, so I got to my knees and prayed, "God, I don't really want to kill myself, but it seems like it would be best for everyone involved. The children are going to get hurt or killed being around me. Susan deserves better than what I can offer her. And I can't go on like this anymore. Please, Jesus, if there is anything You can do, do it, because I am finished here."

No dramatic answer came from heaven in that moment, just the release of my life; I had given up for good. I had said my two cents and now began looking for the convenient opportunity to carry out my suicide plan.

The following Sunday came along without that convenient opportunity presenting itself. I went to church with Susan and the children. As soon as I set foot in the sanctuary, I thought I smelled flowers. There were no flowers in the building, but there was a thick, strong aroma of sweetness in the air that I can only compare to fresh-cut flowers.

We took our seats and I whispered to Susan, "Do you smell that wonderful scent?" She did not.

As we sat listening to the liturgy that last Sunday morning

service in October 2003, each passage made sense to me like never before. Again, like in my teenage years, God was speaking directly to me out of the crowd. But this time it was different than before. I had no "but" to offer God in response to what He was saying. What He said to me that day was so penetrating that it has never left me.

It began with the sweet smell I perceived, that no one else sensed. Days later I sat in amazement as I read the scripture 2 Corinthians 2:14-17. The Bible says that the knowledge of God is like a sweet smelling aroma. I had encountered that sweet aroma as I walked into the sanctuary. God's Spirit had come to me and opened my senses to His presence.

Looking back, I find it interesting how I had loved my own dad's aroma, that sweet smell of working with electronics all day, and here I was enjoying the aroma of my Heavenly Father. The scriptures we read that morning in church, Isaiah 59:21, Mark 10:46-52, and Hebrews 5:11-12, made perfect sense to me, whereas they had not resonated in the past fifteen years of attending church sporadically.

The liturgy spoke the message that God had come to help and be with me and my whole family for generations to come. That my cry for mercy had been heard and answered, opening my eyes to see God for the purpose of following Jesus. The passages hit me in the heart, rather than soaring over my head.

I listened to the story about a blind man named Bartimaeus. This poor old guy kept yelling out to get Jesus' attention, and everyone in the crowd kept telling him to pipe down. But Jesus stopped and told His disciples to bring the blind man to Him. Bartimaeus told Jesus he wanted to be healed. So Jesus healed him, and the former blind man reacted in a way that really impressed me. It rang through me that *I* was Bartimaeus, healed, and that Bartimaeus followed Jesus for the rest of his days. I recalled the perceived call as a teen to be a priest, and that I, according to the third part of the liturgy, should be teaching by now, but that I, Mr. Brilliant ATC man, had been dull-witted and slow to learn. So ironic. I don't recall the sermon that day, but the revelations—sweet aroma, God came to be with me and my family, and following Jesus and teaching other to do the same—were so profound that they became who I still am today. They became my new, unchanging identity in place of the old, changing ATC identity I once knew and fell prey to.

Towards the end of the service, the church conducted a prayer and healing line, something they do during the last Sunday of each month. I did not get up to stand in line and be prayed for, but I couldn't deny something very special was happening to me. I had become so excited by now, that I encouraged Susan to get up and get in the healing line.

During my affair and desperate drug use years, Susan felt she could never do enough to make me happy. Anything she did just didn't seem good enough, no matter how hard she tried. This pushed her to spiral into secret despair. She drank alcohol, a lot, and smoked cigarettes. She was broken, truly broken. Something valuable at church had been given to me and I didn't want her to leave without getting whatever it was too.

She declined. I insisted.

Eventually, she got up and stood in the line of people who wanted to be healed. She said that as she grew closer and closer to the front of the line she became a bit panicked, not knowing what to ask the priest for. Only as it was her turn to be prayed for, as she began stepping forward to the head of the line, only then did understanding hit her and words popped into her mind.

Susan relayed that she understood, deep down and with clarity, at that very moment that she wasn't a total victim. She recalled many of the bad choices she had made, like things she chose to do that she knew would push me away from her, or insisting on her own way. She thought, *I'm sure I could have done things better to preserve the integrity of my marriage and maybe that would have gone a long way in Robert's heart, even to helping him keep his job. But I didn't.* And she recognized that many of her stubborn, self-willed, clearly not-right choices caused those she loved to be in a place of hurt, and brought her to a dark and terrible place of her own. She saw with a penetrating sense of accountability that the misery in her life was her own fault.

That's when the priest asked, "What would you like prayer for?"

Susan replied with the phrase that was only now in her heart and mind, "I want the loving grace of Jesus Christ to take over my life."

He smiled and paused. Then he led her in what we would later learn was a "sinner's prayer." (See page 201.)

She said that his words were the most perfect words she had ever heard, reflecting the exact sentiments that were in her heart. She repeated the words he offered verbatim, through gasps for breath and heavy tears and then returned to her seat. Before the closing benediction, the priest stood before everyone with a huge smile. He looked at Susan for a moment, as if they had a secret. She didn't know what he was smiling about, or why he was looking at her, but she smiled back at him and nodded back in an affirming way.

That's when, still gleaming with joy, he said, "I have an announcement to make! Susan Totman just gave her life to Jesus Christ!"

Susan muttered to me, "I did? Well, that's great!"

Everyone clapped and cheered. The priest pronounced God's blessings upon us all and we left. The service had been amazing, with a sweet smell in the air, those soul-penetrating words to me, and even my wife "giving her life to Jesus," whatever that meant.

That night, my dreams changed—forever. My horrific dreams were turned upside down, as if someone had flipped a coin. The night after attending this service on October 26, 2003, I had my first other-than-nightmare since September 11, 2001. In this new and polar opposite realm of dreaming I saw, simply, "James 1:17," in bold, large letters.

This dream woke me up in the middle of the night. I scrambled for a bedside light, reached for my Bible and looked it up. Now, neither Susan nor I were versed in scripture. I had only just begun reading the Bible. I couldn't have told you if the Book of James was in the Old Testament or the New Testament, much less any specifics about what might be in any particular book of the Bible. So after I finally located James 1:17, I marveled at the words. They seemed to be pulsating with life. What I read in the verse next to it seemed especially relevant to me too:

> Every good and perfect gift is from above, coming down from the Father of the heavenly lights, who does not change like shifting shadows. He chose to give us birth through the word of truth, that we might be a kind of first-fruits of all He created. (James 1:17-18 NIV)

This was my first time experiencing something besides terror in my dreams for more than two years, and it was good! I felt God was saying to me, "My goodness toward you hasn't wavered one iota, ever. *I* Fathered you and that makes you a star!"

What? Me? I was awakened to the truth that God is my Heavenly Father, and He always had good intentions toward me, and they never changed or wavered, regardless of the wretched decisions and course I chose. I was so ashamed, having squandered something so valuable as the incredible gift He had given me as an air traffic controller in the FAA. I climbed out of bed that night, as if "out of my bed of past suffering," and got to my knees, thanking Jesus for healing my eyes, like I had heard in church that day, so that I could see to follow the real Him.

Ever since that day I have enjoyed heavenly dreams, no longer plagued by death in its various horrific living-forms. Now in an opposite fashion the dreams began to reform my life. Not death now, but life!

So, God gave me a sense that He Himself had Fathered me. That would make me a child of God. The very next thing that was revealed to me, within days of the James 1:17 dream, was that God had also made me a man of God. This was nothing less than dumbfounding to me. I realized, at the time, that I wasn't there yet, but the label became a part of me. I saw so clearly that this was my destiny, if you will. Imagine, me a man of God. And in addition, of all things, I heard God calling me a "saint," His "bride," a "sword" in His hand, and on and on He went, transforming my innermost-me into those things I saw through being with Him in His Word. I was a beach bum turned ATC star turned bankrupt, fired, Federal court outcast. Those descriptions I could relate to, but this…this was a totally new mindset.

I had been hating myself for taking away my wife's prospects of a wealthy future. Same with the children. I was so hurt by what I had done to my family; I wanted to make up for all the injury and loss I had caused them, but I knew I could never do that. But God could. In that first year God infused an astonishing hope in me, that if I chose to walk with Jesus, my family would be compensated for my foolishness. He broke away the tremendous sense of shame and guilt I carried. This inner reality helped me believe the rest of what He was saying, "Walk with Me. I will more than make it up to them. I will make living for Me worth your while!"

COURSE CORRECTION

Within two or three days of that pivotal last Sunday in October, an old habit of mine surfaced: going to the medicine cabinet. There, I had morphine-based pain pills that I had been taking every day for years. I opened the cabinet and took ahold of the bottle that first week of this new life. There was a moment of deliberation.

I thought, *Things have been so sweet the last few days. If I take one of these today, it will only be a matter of time before I add Jack Daniels to its effect. And, from there, cocaine. Who knows if or when I will ever come back!*

I was acutely aware of God being right there with me, and in this state of awareness, I had a far out notion that I believe was from God: I had never been addicted to anything; rather, I had been giving myself to the lie that I was addicted. That lie had been broken and the power of addiction with it. I flushed the pills down the toilet, thanking God for rescuing me from needing them ever again.

Was I never physically addicted? I don't know, but I didn't go through any withdrawals. The understanding I gained astonished me, and that understanding gave me such power over the lie of addiction. Relapses? Since 2003, I have had a beer here or a Margarita there. But the lie that I need that type of thing to be happy or satisfied has held no sway over me.

Then suddenly, right after that mystical Sunday, Susan ended up in the hospital. After putting the children to bed one evening, she began feeling chest pain. She describes it as feeling a net around her heart and within that net was a heavy boulder, working through her utter physical agony, to pull her heart down and out of her chest. She hoped she'd wake the next day feeling better and went to bed. She felt the same the next morning but went to work anyway. The pain persisted. She finally left work before her lunch break and drove herself to the emergency room.

The doctors were unable to make a diagnosis, so they put her on IVs to help with her pain and admitted her for observation and tests. While Susan was on heavy meds in the hospital bed, the phone rang. It was my aunt, one of my favorites, actually. But my aunt didn't call Susan simply to check on her health. When she heard that Susan was hospitalized with chest pain, she was compelled to share that she knew more about me than she had ever admitted to Susan before.

When I was torn between the two women, I introduced the other woman to some of my relatives, including this particular, favorite aunt. The other woman was wearing a nice diamond ring I had given her. I was planning to leave Susan and marry this woman, and my aunt knew it. My concerned aunt believed that I was killing Susan (whom she loved) and felt like now, more than ever, Susan needed to know that

I had been unfaithful. As if, "Robert is doing this to you with all this stress, and you need to know that he has been unfaithful too so you can decide if you are willing to allow him to keep treating you this way or not." She wanted whatever was hurting Susan to stop, even if it meant getting her away from me.

Susan said that my aunt's phone call only confirmed what she already knew deep down in her heart. She confronted me on this issue for the final time, "Did you have an affair? Don't lie to me. Tell me the truth. Place your trash before me and let me decide what to do with you from there."

Now with an acute awareness of the presence of Almighty God, for the first time I could not lie. There in the hospital room, I admitted to her that I had been carrying on an affair for quite some time, but had ended it in the spring of that year, choosing her and my family. I wept while she beat me with a box of Kleenex. Her heart was certainly broken and her face showed much anger, streaming with tears. What? This was "the loving grace of Jesus Christ taking over my life" that she had asked for?

The doctors couldn't find out what was causing Susan's chest pain. But I knew. I had broken her heart, and the only way it could begin to heal was for the truth of my affair to be exposed. Susan was released from the hospital to begin her own recovery process, in more ways than one. That first couple of weeks of me knowing God, I was in hot water while Susan was being forced to deal with a terrible thing that I had no excuse for bringing into our lives.

Neither of us knew what to do or how to cope with our raw reality. All I could do was pour my heart out to my newfound God—so much regret and sorrow, fresh accountability for the devastation, and pleas for His help. I would kneel at my bedside with an open Bible before me and just say to God everything that I was feeling. Susan didn't want anything to do with me at this point, or to hear a single word from me either. So it's not like cooking dinner to show her I was sorry would have been acceptable. She wanted me away from her, and instead of begging her otherwise, I did the only other thing I knew to do—go to God. With my more developed understanding now, I see that where I was weak and powerless, I couldn't have done anything more effective or right. Instead of trying to change her mind, in hindsight I see that I went to the only thing (One) who could do anything—God.

The dreams and words I encountered each day worked to comfort and lift me, even while Susan seemed to be entombed beneath the excruciating weight of my sinful actions. It was weird. There was a separation of sorts taking place that went beyond what either of us understood. God was coming between us, kind of like a glue to hold us together. He was pressing Himself to be the center of attention, a way for us to obtain healing and be drawn together. I mean, we had both invited Him to have His way, and He was.

Susan says everywhere she looked in the Bible during that time, all she saw was adultery. She even slammed her Bible shut in exasperation, "Is there anything else in this Book of Yours, God?" Apparently, He was not willing to move on with her until she could get together with God on the topic, seeing things the way He wanted her to see them.

He empowered me to trust Him through specific verses like, "The LORD is close to the brokenhearted and saves those who are crushed in spirit." Mind you, I did not go looking for these types of verses but they were presented to me—through a daily devotional or an encouraging word from someone at church, or the like, and they echoed in the air as witnessed through my dreams. All I could do was trust this new Presence in my life. I could do nothing more. I was completely powerless, but for these relevant words in which to place my confidence.

For months, I would be awakened in the middle of the night by various songs and sounds of praise to God. It was totally other-worldly! I'm saying that the loudest praise to God would awaken me from my sleep at 1:00 a.m. or 2:00 a.m. or 3:00 a.m. I would respond by springing out of bed, kneeling beside it and joining in what I was hearing, verbalizing the same, and I couldn't possibly keep up with the passionate, fervent, loud praise either. No one else in our house could hear the praise but me, it was so loud in my heart and mind.

Those first weeks I noticed feeling almost lighter than air because all of the weights of my misery were simply gone. Shame and guilt were gone. Defeat was gone. Hopelessness was no more, all of a sudden. And so on. This helped to inspire the praise. The praise was a response to experiencing Truth. I was being trained to pay more attention to these brand new other-worldly perceptions than to my feelings or what I saw in my circumstances. As if God was saying, "Don't look there! Pay attention to Me (this new sight)."

And He was so evident all of a sudden. I could so clearly

sense God, His Person. I was keenly aware that He was real and that He was right there with me. I could hear Him speaking to me, various expressions of love and hope. His Person became so pronounced to me that even when He wasn't speaking to me, I could feel Him near and even listening to my thoughts. I realize that sounds weird, but, again, I am not sharing an opinion (as the subsequent fruit of our lives will bear out). I'm sharing what actually happened to me.

But to go back to those earliest days, I was experiencing God's love, but far from complete, because my wife was being crushed right before my eyes. She had been hospitalized and then traumatized by the reality of my affair, and was struggling with the aftermath. One evening, around ten days after that eye-opening last Sunday in October, 2003, I stood alone on the back porch of our home, praying. Now I knew without a doubt that God was real and loved me, that He was indeed Almighty and present. I said, "Father, I don't want a divorce, but that's exactly what I deserve. I think I can go on now without killing myself because of Your presence in my life. So whatever You decide is fine with me. I think I can do it, because I know You are with me." I was giving Him my marriage and inviting His control of its outcome. I had but a mere glimmer of hope in this matter of going on without her and not killing myself.

I knew undoubtedly that God was real and loved me, but the notion of getting through life without Susan at my side was a daunting, intimidating notion indeed. I couldn't fathom living without her or putting the children through the misery I endured as a child because of divorce. With the tiniest measure of belief, I declared my will to God and purposed to go on, with Him, no matter the outcome.

At that moment, Susan opened the back door of our home and said to me, "I've thought about it and decided I will try to forgive you. We will try to work this out." And without waiting for me to answer, she returned indoors, closing the door. She had not heard my prayer to God and I was astonished to say the least. God, who had come to so powerfully impact my life, was beginning to touch the lives of those closest to me and was mercifully answering my heart's desire.

It was as if corridors had been opened in the heavens and I had direct access to God. I didn't know the terms or notions at the time, only that, over the next many months, God was showing me His point of view, that He sees the Church (His children) in kick-butt mode, with Him doting over us and backing us up in every way. That He loves people and He thinks about us non-stop and fantasizes about different ways to shower us with expressions of love. His affection for people is relentless. That new awareness of His presence became my inspiration to clean myself up from drugs and alcohol. I didn't want to offend the sweet Presence that was delighted in even me.

I went to the Bible constantly. As a kid I didn't like school, didn't do well in it either. And now I couldn't get enough of studying. Each time I went to God's Word, I felt as though I was having an actual meeting with God. As an air traffic controller I had the uncanny ability to speak by the book, fluently. I see now how that was God's gift to me, and I mismanaged it. But by God's grace, He is giving my gifting a new purpose. Now while I'm preaching or sharing God's word, most often I can literally see the pages of the Bible in my mind's eye. Just like I could memorize and maintain multiple, complex air traffic routes, my mind recalls the scriptures clearly: book, chapter and verse. It's like reading from memory, and I am aware that His presence is intricately involved.

During these voracious months of Bible reading, I received a certain knowing that if I didn't spend the rest of my life looking deeper and deeper into God's Word, I would have wasted my time here on earth. This sense carried the notion that I had been placed upon a lifetime scholarship, if you will, to look more and more into God's Word. Could it be that everything I would ever need would be provided so that I could fellowship with God through His Word? A fully paid scholarship from heaven just to get to know God more and more? I wondered.

I would spend time in the Bible and then experience vivid, life-infusing dreams about the topics which I had just studied. Or, I would dream of astonishing things and then open my Bible "at random" the next morning to the very thing I had just personally experienced through lucid dreams. Again, words were being presented to me that validated the dreams, whether through a morning devotional, a sermon on TV, a word through a friend or the like. I wasn't hunting for some biblical thing to justify my impressions; rather, biblical things were just appearing to me from here or there that echoed the dreams, justifying themselves to me as authentic. These sequences were happening nearly every single day, providing me with a compass by which I could begin to think straight, consistently, through focusing on these things above all else.

I'd possessed an apparent mystical intuitiveness while working traffic. Even my co-workers commented on my other-worldly ability to foresee events during live, developing ATC situations. It was actually eerie to see disasters averted because of a decision and action that I made before it became apparent that a disaster had been developing. I used to think God was answering the prayers of flight passengers. Perhaps this "intuition" to give God credit has something to do with these dreams and insights I was experiencing, as if they have been with me all along. But now I was experiencing a back and forth, two-way communication.

The scripture and my dreams were one, echoing like a ringing bell as I let go of my past and all of the shame I had brought upon myself and my innocent family. My receptiveness to the Bible study in conjunction with the redeemed dreams began to reform me; that is, change who I was.

But after Susan announced her decision to try and forgive me so that we could work things out, I had a fear. I was so exuberant about my new, undeniable access to God, but my precious Susan was still languishing under the horrendous weight of depravity that I had brought into our home and placed upon her. I felt as though I had been walking in the clouds, whereas my wife was suffering so terribly. I felt so rich, but I didn't want to be void of compassion toward her through my own personal wealth. I feared pride, so I prayed one morning while showering, "Humble me, Father. Don't let me become proud because of all of this extraordinary wealth You are sharing with me."

Three days after our encounter on the porch, my wife experienced God in a life-altering way. On Friday, November

7, 2003, nearly two weeks after Susan's healing prayer at church, Susan went to the bank after work. A few days earlier she had heard from a long lost cousin who had searched her out and called her, then invited our family for a visit. Her cousin's family had moved away when Susan was a young child, and they had lost touch with each other. Susan had wondered about her cousin over the years, and during that first phone call, Susan learned they had both given their lives to Jesus on the same recent Sunday!

A check had arrived in the mail from a life insurance policy we'd cashed in, and Susan needed that check to be cashed so we could afford to drive to her cousin's home, an hour and a half drive from where we lived in Florida. So she went to the bank, hoping to cash the check, but doubting they would release the funds immediately since it was an out-of-state check. Susan's encounter with God began in the drive-through teller service.

As she waited for the teller to process and most likely put a hold on the check, Susan became awestruck by realities that she could hardly believe were real, yet couldn't deny, "signs" that the two women working at the drive-through window were sisters in Christ. Suddenly translucent flames appeared over the women's heads. (We would only later learn that such a thing is in the Bible.) Her heart filled with an overflowing love she had never even felt toward family before, much less strangers. She felt a strong sense of long-lost sisters found, and she thought, *So this is what God sees when He looks at us–irresistible perfection and close-knit family!* She marveled at the insights. That's when the teller chimed in over the speaker and said, "Everything is fine, Mrs. Totman.

You can withdraw these funds right away if you'd like to."

Susan thanked the teller and began to drive away, thinking, *God must have done that!* She began thanking Jesus for the favor He gave her at the bank, and for whatever that was that she had just seen, felt and experienced. (By the way, a month later we went inside the bank and shared these things with those two ladies. Both of the women confessed to being Christians.) At the time, Susan wasn't sure if she should tell me about what she had seen and felt; it seemed so bizarre, and she wondered if I might have her committed to an institution if she shared these never-even-remotely-considered perceptions with me.

Susan stopped at a red light as she was leaving the bank parking lot, when all of a sudden she saw the face of Jesus. His face filled her entire field of vision; it was huge! The light changed to green and, looking through this astonishing, translucent sight, she began to drive. She cried out, "Lord, thank You for coming to see me! There's a whole universe and billions and billions of people, and You would come to see me? You make me feel like I matter to You! Thank You for coming to see me. Thank You for saving me! Thank You for giving me favor at the bank!" The words gushed out of her mouth. Then, the more she tried to speak, more and more waves of love and power and understanding of who He is began to reverberate through her, stifling her ability to say anything at all and even taking her breath away.

As she shared all this with me after she arrived home, she told me, "I don't know that I've ever cried from such a deep place of my soul. I just wanted Him to know that He made me feel so honored. I felt so little. I felt like I didn't mean anything compared to Him. But He showed me that I meant the whole world to Him. I felt Him saying, 'You are perfect for Me. I love you so much!'"

She laughed as she shared with me how she merely thought her words to Jesus while she was driving, "I told Him, 'I'm driving! Jesus, I'm driving! You've got to let me get home alive!'" And of course her thoughts went to our family: "I asked Jesus, 'Please don't let anything bad happen to my family.' And He replied to that too, saying that our family would be just fine. In fact, He said He would use us to impact and change many, many lives with His Word through His love.

"Robert, I don't even know how, but I was in, and doing, two totally different things at the very same time! He came down and visited me!" My wife's eyes sparkled with new life. She wasn't out of her mind; she was having an encounter with God Most High! I had been concerned that I wouldn't be compassionate toward her, asking Him to humble me, and this is how He answered my prayer.

Now Susan and I were united as one in Christ. This healing revelation of God empowered Susan to stick with her earlier choice to forgive me and then embark upon the journey of growing into that choice. The husband had his eyes opened for the purpose of following Jesus, and the wife received a commission to tell others of the things we had, and would, personally witness about God as He "sends us" to and fro, united in Him. God made it to where Susan and I needed each other to express the whole of His will for us.

That night we called our priest to have Susan report her bizarre events to him, to find out from someone who would know if she was actually going crazy or not. He calmed us down, saying that he had heard of such things before, and asked her to write it all down without skipping any details. He said he would like to have a copy of what she wrote. She did as he instructed. We went to the Saturday morning prayer meeting at church and, not seeing the priest there that day, she placed what she had written on his desk. We were pleasantly surprised Sunday morning when he read what she wrote as his sermon. Many were weeping. When he finished reading, he asked Susan if she had anything to add. She stood in front of the crowd and shared from her heart and her new understanding, how terribly we had all been totally missing the point of how much God loves us all.

A good friend once told us, "God loves us perfectly right where we are and too much to leave us there." We carry heartfelt love for the people in that church and still maintain contact with some of them to this day, however a mere six months later we would leave that denomination with the priest's blessing on our unfolding adventure of following Jesus.

LIVING IN THE CLOUDS

Having our marriage healed did restore blissful intimacy between Susan and me. In fact, nine months from the day that Susan encountered Jesus at the bank, Dr. Christian was on call to deliver our new baby, Grace.

During the weekdays through the first seven months of her pregnancy, Susan continued to work at a cell phone company as a type of office manager. Her appetite for God matched mine. She would read her Bible and pray each morning and then, enveloped with a Christ-centered atmosphere, bring encouragement to her work place each day. At the time, it was a place filled with much bickering and backbiting. This broke her heart. She would frequent the restroom at work to kneel and pray for God to change things for the better. He kept her full of His presence. People would visit her at her desk, saying, "I just want to sit near you. There's something about the air around you that is calming and sweet."

While Susan was pregnant with our third child, I filled my days with time on my knees in prayer, with a Bible opened before me all day every day. I read in the Bible that whoever says he abides in Him (Christ) ought to walk in the same way in which He walked. (I John 2:6). That means living like Jesus did. Jesus didn't say or do anything apart from first hearing God the Father say it or see Him doing it, so it only made sense to me that I should talk with God before I started out on my day.

In those early months I spent three, six, eight hours per day on my knees. My bedroom door remained open. I spent hours upon hours quiet and still, kneeling before God's open Word. There was a heavy peace, rest and order upon our whole house. About a month after I came to know the Lord, a strong silence came over me that lasted a month. I was hugely quieted. I didn't pray out loud. I had next to nothing to say to anyone. It was part of my new formation, carried out without any conscious effort. I was just enjoying being so secure, so assured.

After that month, I did begin praying out loud again and resumed normal conversations. But my day-to-day activity was mostly secluded study time–being wowed. Once or twice a week, I would take the children to see Susan at work for all of us to have lunch together. The children and I would have meaningful interludes together on and off through the days. I would come to them and spill out this astonishing, unconditional, abandoned love and approval upon them. Or they would come to me, while I knelt bedside, and climb up my back onto the bed while I giggled with them. I loved it! Their tiny little hands, knees and elbows felt like a free massage to my back, and I would wrap them up in my arms, upon the bed, and love on them, or they would curl up within my arms which were formed to pray, and just lie there quietly while I read the Word aloud, prayed to God, or prayed over them. Then they'd use my back for a slide and retreat from the bedroom, back on their way to play–all filled up with Daddy's love. They were with me, but filled with Him.

As with my ATC training, I thoroughly enjoyed and utterly consumed all of this agreeable material—the Bible—completely. I began living a new wide-open lifestyle, and studied with a newfound passion and zeal. This solid foundation of daily prayer and Bible study and journaling has carried itself all the way through our journey to this very day. It's my meeting time with God. I find that when the meeting is over, I remain surrounded by Him all day long, watching the things we discussed unfold before me. I must admit that I now rarely spend six or more hours a day on my knees in prayerful study, winnowing my perceptions as I did then. But I do still spend several hours each morning within these same disciplines. Anything I've done right or well is because of God's ever-drawing grace to me. It's His relentless kindness that keeps me coming back.

But we also learned quickly that humanity has an enemy, a trespasser in the spirit realm who troubles mankind for the purpose of destroying everything that is pleasing to God. Our enemy is none other than the serpent known as the devil. When we first learned about this enemy, we thought, *What? Our God-given new life still has a deceiving snake in it? No way!* Then we began to recognize the enemy's visits.

One night, early in our new lives, we were resting in bed and about to fall asleep. Susan asked, "Do you ever think about her?" She was referring to the other woman. Turns out Susan had been lying there in utter peace when all of a sudden she began experiencing a bombardment of mental sights, seeing me and the other woman in the sack together doing all sorts of things that are only meant for the marriage bed.

Unaware of this, I responded, "Why do you ask?"

She shared with me what she had been seeing in her mind's eye.

In the gravity of the moment, I responded soberly by sharing with her that for the last few minutes I was being flooded with memories of being in bed with the other woman. I told her of my regret, apologized yet again, and shared with Susan that I was not enjoying the memories, and that I had been actively resisting them, along with all of their associated feelings of guilt and shame, as I laid there silently wishing to go to sleep.

Humanity's enemy hates marriage because holy matrimony pleases God. In fact, God's enemy hates all unity among people. Even the smallest household is the target of real, authentic demonic attacks. The enemy had come to divide us and set us against one another that night.

There is a poignant analogy of how the real enemy works in a scene out of the movie, *The Avengers*. The heroes (representing children of God) who are charged to save the planet from mankind's enemy are in a lab room aboard an airborne aircraft carrier. The Tesseract (a supernatural power representing the serpent) sits on a desk, mounted upon a scepter (representing rule). This power is silent, merely in the room. As the life-saving heroes speak to one another, their conversation is being influenced by the evil power in the room. They do not recognize the evil power's influence over their conversation and begin to criticize one another and suspect one another of having bad motives. It isn't long before they are challenging one another to all-out fight, to destroy each other.

Likewise, an evil influence had entered our home that night and it was seeking to pit Susan and me against one another. Because of our new-found grace of God, we recognized what was going on and turned to Him for help. We agreed that God had forgiven our sins, we had forgiven each other, and that we were both brand new, guiltless creations.

Susan and I were not unfamiliar with enemy attacks. We'd lived in dangerous, racist areas of Puerto Rico and had survived the vicious terrorist attacks of 9/11. We recognized that the people—our neighbors on the island and the radical-Muslims—were not the ones attacking us; rather, it was the same evil spirit who was behind their actions. With God's help, we were not going to sit back and let the enemy win this time. Within moments we were telling the evil entity that it was a trespasser and not welcomed in our marriage or home, saying, "In the Name of Jesus Christ, get out!" We then thanked God for His faithfulness and enjoyed a peaceful night's sleep together.

It didn't occur to us in those early days just how much rest we needed to prepare for what was ahead. Actually, we didn't have an inkling of what God had in store for us. We were just living our lives with Him the best way we knew how. We were having "crazy" sights of "reality" that took our attention away from what most people would be concerned with, like "What are you going to do with your life? And "How are you going to dig yourself out of the ditch you got yourself into?" God kept pouring it on with amazing sights of heavenly things to carry us forward without the weight of hows and whys.

One night, I had a dream in which I saw an open Bible and heard, "Prepare the way for the Lord!" At that statement, the Bible slammed closed (from the end to the beginning; that is, from back to front) with a thunderous thud. The thud was accompanied by a rushed statement, "Jesus is coming!" These dramatic events woke me from my dream with a gasp of air. I reached over to Susan who was sleeping next to me, placed my hand upon her, and woke her.

"Honey, I just had a dream that Jesus is coming. Like today!"

"That's nice," she replied, and went right back to sleep, as did I.

Before too long, she woke me, "Robert! I just had a dream that shouted, 'Prepare ye the way of the LORD!' He's coming so soon, Robert. Like any time now!"

As if this wasn't enough, just like so many other mornings, our Bible study that morning included passages that clearly echoed our spiritual perceptions. Again, not that we would go searching for passages that reflected our dreams, but the topic of our daily devotional or the page we happened to open to would be absolute mirrors of what had been "revealed" to us. These profound, consistent occurrences utterly arrested us.

God revealed to both of us the urgency of the times and His imminent return. "So, what do we do now?" we asked each other. "Do we go around like madmen, warning of Christ's return everywhere we go, with every breath, and holding signs that say The End Has Come! on street corners?" Of course not, we determined. Love is not overbearing. God meets people where they are. Instead of hounding people in an overbearing way, obnoxiously relaying the urgency of this matter, we found peace trusting in God's love to do the persuading. Intense urgency balanced with trust and love became part of our new identity, part of who we are and why we do the things we do. It's a major part of what makes us tick.

Our closest relatives and those people we regularly were in contact with began to see the changes in our lives. Family members who professed to be Christians had been praying for us, because of our recent 9/11, pending-divorce circumstances. They had been watching a terrible thing unfold. Susan's dad, who lived in Louisiana at the time and is deceased now, had received Christ as his Savior after coming home from Vietnam, but rather than experiencing dramatic supernatural help, suffered alcoholism, divorce and then only a small measure of help. My mom, too, professed Christianity, but bore little fruit to distinguish from someone who did not. These people were witnesses of our plight. They were watching our demise and praying for us. And then it was like a God-bomb had hit and we were like a whole different type of Ground Zero. God had answered their prayers.

Many started yielding to the Spirit that was transforming our own hearts and attitudes. All around us, more and more people were choosing to follow Jesus. Susan's dad and my mom, within about two months, became absolutely sold out to Jesus. They turned into Jesus freaks (respectfully). Susan's dad passed head over heels in love with Jesus, telling just about everyone he came into contact with about the Lord.

My mom, too, is like a Jesus-megaphone to this very day.

Within weeks of the ground zero heavenly blast, people from church began to call us at home to speak with us and hear what we had to say. My dad is an intellect. For years, his intellect impeded his surrender to Jesus, until after watching our first two years in the Lord. From his mathematician mind, he said, "It's as if you have won the lottery three times a week for two years!" Logically, he surrendered his all to Jesus.

Then we began to see a change even with some of the on-lookers and naysayers who thought we were crazy. Some of our relatives were 100 percent opposed to our new life. Odd, you'd think that if they loved us they would be happy that things were changing for the better. But apparently we were not changing in a way that was pleasing to them. It took a few years, but eventually, one by one, those who openly opposed us returned to us, seeking us out to give God glory. "I thought you were crazy, but now I see that you are not."

Then Jesus delivered the heaviest message to me He'd given so far. As I awoke one morning, I heard His voice as clearly as I've ever heard the voice of God:

"Put the weight of your world upon My shoulders, and I will put My weight upon your world."

I giggled, replying, "I don't have any weight, Lord." You see, we were thoroughly living in the clouds, sort-of-speaking, at this time. I honestly didn't feel the weight of any burdens.

I did come to understand that I was being instructed to cast my cares (should any develop) upon Christ, my sins upon Him, to roll my desires and any burdening thing over and onto His shoulders. Even the weighty things that most people would consider good, like being a homeowner or having an esteemed job title. His promise to me that morning was that if I would faithfully, with His help, cast my weight (generally, negative things but including things that gave me a sense of self value too) upon Him, He would in exchange put His weight (mercy, honor, awe) upon my world. My response, then, worked both ways, "I don't have any weight, Lord." No cares. No esteem either. And no job. What about that?

TESTING MY WINGS

About two weeks before baby Grace was due, still living in the duplex condo we'd purchased after I'd returned to Susan, we prayerfully concluded that God would take care of us, and Susan quit her job. She had been working since before I cashed in my 401K. We were like God's babies ourselves, freshly breaking out of something very dark. God had us in a special place, close to His heart, in our new journey, clearly leading us and healing our battered souls. I sought God all day every day. This was my rehab, formation of new habits, my reformation of sorts.

I know it sounds crazy and difficult for some to believe, but we were (and are) fully convinced that God would take care of us somehow. We both heard from God that He would meet our needs, and that we were not to concern ourselves over money. In fact, God was calling us to NOT seek employment at the time, but to trust Him, to give Him the opportunity to show us He was faithful and that He would provide for us.

It was very private and very personal. When we had fears about income, for instance, we would quickly receive the strongest rebuke from God. Not a harsh rebuke, but a deep, assuring insistent voice, "I am Your Father, Creator of the Universe, Your Provider!" quieting us in trustful reverence. I had read in the book of Job that God stops every man from his work so he can look up and get to know God, his Provider. That's what happened to me after 9/11. Over time I learned to trust Him completely, always remaining open to whatever God wanted me to do. I've repeatedly prayed, "If You want me to have a job, I'm here for You to send me."

I did apply for a job at Home Depot and McDonald's, receiving employment from neither. Overqualified? I don't know, but I do believe with all of my heart that I applied for those jobs in unbelief. I sought those jobs as a means to take care of my family, while God was saying that He would take care of us Himself.

It so happens that our baby, Grace, was delivered by Dr. Christian on a Sunday at the Baptist Hospital, nine months from the day that Christ appeared to Susan at the bank. We were greatly encouraged by this alignment of events. I mean, really, Dr. Christian? On a Sunday? We thought he could have been playing golf on his day off, the Sabbath, of all days. And, nine months from the day? Was Jesus saying He had become our Bank Account? God had been good to us.

When Grace was six weeks old, Susan had a heavenly encounter in a dream. A messenger clothed in light appeared to her, speaking. He was at a distance, as if across a large room, and walking toward her. With each and every step toward her and each word spoken to her he grew brighter, transforming from the figure of a somewhat glowing man to eventually becoming so bright that he was unbearably brilliant to look at. All of this took place as he said, "The harvest is plentiful but the workers are few. You have been tested and passed the test. Now you are being promoted!" The final two words accompanied the culmination of brilliant light that forced her to withdraw, in a sense, from the encounter as she snapped out of the dream. She lay awake in utter amazement, contemplating this, when she heard the sweetest, tiny whisper. Lying right there next to Susan, infant Grace had spoken a sentence! The six-week-old infant did the impossible when she spoke in her sleep, saying, "We should not fear, but have faith." We would later learn that this sentiment is the most repeated instruction in the Bible (to not be afraid).

Again, our morning Bible study happened to mirror Susan's dream. We'd learned we couldn't obey dreams without consulting God's Word, impartially, without being swayed by our dreams. To follow dreams alone could be crazy. We recorded in our journals all the times our daily devotions mirrored events such as these. God was doing some *serious* prompting.

Shortly thereafter, things began to look bleak in the natural realm of our finances. We had no source of income and were not advertising our actions to anyone, because we felt we were in so deep with the Lord regarding our circumstances that most people couldn't possibly relate. We rolled our cares upon the Lord, inspired by Him, even as I still somewhat struggled with my responsibility to provide for my family. I was doing the best that I could to trust that God had a plan for our provision, and He was faithfully flooding us with what we needed to believe.

Actually, we weren't smart enough to recognize that God might be calling us to full time ministry. Or maybe He was intentionally keeping our eyes closed to the call to ministry until it was time for us to see. Rather, God was just so big in our faces and telling us that everything was going to be great. We didn't see everything going great in the natural at all, and there was some struggle with that. But, as I said previously, when we doubted, thinking I should look for a job, God would answer firmly, "No" and to trust in Him.

So, He was saying it would be okay. I was spending lots of time on my knees, in His Word. I was enjoying a phenomenal, real relationship with a Person who was there visiting with me. And then I tried to reconcile that reality with the family needs that my eyes were seeing. He was wooing us into submission; His reality for us was more real than what we were seeing. Again, we did not have the wherewithal to even consider fulltime ministry, even though that's exactly what He was showing me. Weird how one can see so much and see nothing at all at the same time.

Then seemingly random checks started to come to us, unsolicited. These worked to affirm my private time with God, finally connecting our natural circumstances with all of those spiritual perceptions about Him providing. One check even arrived to our Florida home with our old New York address on it. I had been deep in prayer and God's Word, "Father, how are we going to do this? How are we going to get by?"

I was impressed, "You will eat from My hand for the rest of your days." I had an image in my mind of the whole wide world in His hand and began leaning toward the notion that we were going to be just fine. When I asked God how this would happen, I heard, "From the kindness and generosity of the saints." Hmmm.... We were frantic for finances when I heard that, and I wasn't sure if my own reasoning may have been clouding up my spiritual hearing. So I called a praying friend for help.

This friend was a random guy from the pews at the small Episcopal Church where Susan and I had been attending. Back at the height of our crisis, he heard about our dramatic recent events and life story, about my up-close experiences on 9/11 and our pending divorce, and he began praying for us. And he never stopped. He wasn't all up in our faces, but prayed from afar. Once or twice a month he would give us a daily devotional or a few words of advice. His approach was exactly what I needed. The Spirit of God was upon me so richly that I didn't have a compulsion to ask people many questions. But every now and then I would ask him or a person in authority within the church a question to gauge if I was crazy or not.

This man and his wife were (and are) prayer warriors, very well versed in spiritual realities. The Lord gave me a sight one time that this guy was holding a sniper rifle and using it like a pro, representing the effectiveness of his prayers.

When I called this prayer sniper friend, I didn't share our financial burden, but I did tell him what I thought I had heard from God, about Him providing for us, asking, "What do you make of that?"

He chuckled and replied, "God told me to put $1,000 aside for you. Would you like it in cash? A check? Gold?"

In that same week, another man called us from across

the country. We had not spoken to him in about a year, and we had not shared any of the details of our lives with him, other than informing him that we had met Jesus. He reported that he had been in agony for nearly three days, wrestling with God. He said that God told him to give us a significant sum of money, but that he didn't see how he could obey. Finally, he reported, he found peace with God by agreeing to send the amount spread out over twelve monthly offerings, asking, "If that would be okay with you."

"Okay with us? Wow! Of course, thank you so much for obeying God!"

By the time Grace was about two months old, God's promise of provision was so real, vibrant and rich to us that I called the Salvation Army to volunteer, not apply for a job, for their Christmas Angel Tree Program that gathers toys for needy children. Here we were merely scraping by, but we knew we were rich because of the extravagant grace we were experiencing. On my third day of volunteering a head honcho from the organization approached me and offered me a full time job with full benefits. The organization's leaders had been watching me joyously work. He told me that they had been praying for God to send them the right person for a specific opening, Disaster Relief Coordinator for NE Florida, and he believed I was an answer to their prayer. At the time I really couldn't care less what the job title was. It was full time employment, my first since being fired, and included health benefits for my whole family. Only looking back now do I see how the next twelve months were in preparation to give up everything to follow Jesus. We were growing into the vision Susan had which revealed our promotion into the harvest field and needed time to digest that our infant had spoken–and what she had said.

God seemed to be leading me into this employment, and was also still providing for our family in other ways. While I gathered toys for needy children that year, we did not have enough money to buy Christmas presents for our three children. We spent all that we had to give into the Angel Tree Program. It turns out, without soliciting help our children were flooded with loving Christmas presents from near and far that year. It was their largest Christmas to that date, even bigger than when I was in the FAA. Perhaps it's related that a few years later, God provided a saint in our lives who determined to buy all of our children many Christmas gifts every year.

I began working full time at the Salvation Army in downtown Jacksonville, FL, at the social services building, a homeless shelter, and a halfway house. At one-year-old in Christ, this was a ripe field for me. My heart went out to the people in this place, where many were ordered by the court to live, in somewhat relaxed confinement, while they underwent drug or alcohol rehabilitation, and others came for immediate emergency relief via food and shelter. God's unconditional, non-condemning love rushed through me to all those who would have it. There's no doubt that my drug and alcohol past helped me put myself in their skin (one biblical definition of mercy) and meet them right where they were. God had placed me among these people who were struggling with the same demons I had succumbed to for so many years, and He was using my past and current state to bring them hope that they firmly latched onto.

The addicts who were being healed took to me and the message I brought with tenacity. I often heard, "I've never heard the Gospel like!" It was recovering drug-addicts and reforming prostitutes who first called me "pastor." I declined the title, but they would say, "Well, you're my pastor no matter what you say!" (Interestingly, the same chapter of scripture, Hebrews 5, that struck me so deeply on my first day in the Lord that fateful Sunday says that no person takes this honor, of teaching God's Word, upon himself.)

One of my duties included managing a cafeteria that provided dinner to the homeless each night. I joined the staff in serving food in the chow line, and after everyone had been served, mingled with the crowd for a while. Then I would give a ten to fifteen minute heartfelt word of encouragement, holding an open Bible in my hands and referring to it. Afterward, people would approach me for prayer or counsel. I prayed for them, and we grew together.

I recall one evening that after serving lima beans and rice, I gave a fiery word from my heart and then offered individual prayer or counsel as usual. A man approached me with heavy tears streaming down his face and loads of snot dripping from his nose. He was covered in vomit and the smell of urine was all over him. Without any prompting from me, he fervently claimed Christ as his Savior and, right in front of me, asked Jesus to be his Lord forever, verbalizing what I heard to be heartfelt confidence that Jesus would never leave such a request unanswered.

In this newfound love that I was walking within, without reservation or hesitation, I grabbed him in a moment of delight and we enjoyed a long and heartfelt hug together—snot, vomit, urine and all. Later, I marveled at the work God had done in me, to love in this way. Apart from God's influence I can't say that I would ever have hugged a person in such a state. That man became part of those I tended to personally each day.

This became my first congregation, apart from my family at home. There was mutual love and respect among us, which included no judgment. They seemed to understand that certain behaviors were not good, and when they came around me those things were not an issue. We were together to hear about the Living God. It was absolutely joyful, with many giving their lives to Jesus.

I also trained on, and took charge of, the Salvation Army's disaster relief mobile food truck. This was a blow to my ego. I had gone from working as an air traffic controller to now driving what I felt others would call a "roach coach." It wasn't a roach coach—it was clean—but I had to work through what I perceived to be a vast demotion. I kept telling myself that I was walking in the greatest reward the earth had to offer: I was a child of God and there is no higher honor that can be had here on earth. I rolled the weight of "job title" over onto Jesus' shoulders, exchanging it for whatever weight—be it mercy or honor or awe at His amazing accomplishments—He would put upon my world.

One of the ways that Jesus put His weight upon my world took place when a man came in a wheelchair to be served. We chatted. He told me that he had been bound to the wheelchair for twenty-two years. That night after work, when I got home, I prayed for him. Then I had a dream that he got up out of his wheelchair and began walking.

After spending time in prayer and God's Word the next morning, I returned to work and he was there again. We chatted some more. I asked him, "Do you think God could heal you and raise you up from that wheelchair?"

He replied, "I suppose, one day. If He wanted to."

I said, "What if He wanted to two weeks ago?"

He was stumped. I offered to pray for him, asserting that we would ask God right now to heal him so that he wouldn't need the wheelchair anymore. He agreed. I placed my hands on his shoulders and prayed. No miracle. We didn't know what to think. I told him not to worry about it and, together, we gave praise to God anyway.

That night, when I got home, I sought the Lord some more, "What's up with that, Lord? I thought You said You would heal him, that he would get up and walk?"

Before I left for work the next day, after more prayer and Bible study, I was certain that God was saying He would cause the man to get up and walk. When I got to work, there he was again. After chatting a bit, I said, "Let's pray again, for your healing." He agreed. I did just as I had done before, placing my hands upon his shoulders and praying from my heart, according to what I believed God had revealed to me.

Nothing.

But this time the man seemed to have a rebellious heart toward the wheelchair, "No! I believe God can heal me and wants to right now!"

He struggled to stand up, but couldn't quite get out of the chair. It was Friday night. We parted ways. As I sat at my desk Monday morning that same man came strolling into my office on his own two feet, with a magnificent smile gracing his face, and the wheelchair nowhere in sight. He said that he couldn't get over my Friday evening prayers, and that he refused not to be healed by God. He said he just kept trying to get up and walk and that, eventually, Friday night he was up and walking around. He saw his doctor too, who told him to knock it off before he hurt himself, but that he was determined to get his healing from God. He continued coming to the social services, happy as can be on his own two feet, for a few weeks, and then he went away, praising God.

As the Disaster Relief Coordinator for our branch of Northeast Florida for the Salvation Army, I was in charge of the vast warehouse of disaster relief supplies as well as the food truck. That's when Hurricane Katrina struck the Gulf Coast in August of 2005. First, I was working in New York on 9/11 and now here I was on the Gulf Coast to pick up the pieces of another national disaster. The wind and water brought damage like I had never seen before, wiping out massive swaths of trees and buildings. Christ placed more of His weight, his awe, upon my world. Two or three days before the storm struck New Orleans, I had a dream in which I saw the damage to the Superdome that everyone else saw on TV in the days after the storm struck. The morning of this dream, God's Spirit ministered to me, "My righteousness is going before you to prepare the way."

Before the storm hit, the Salvation Army mobilized help from all over America, and our NE Florida unit joined a convoy converging upon the area from the Southeastern United States. We drove as far as we could safely drive toward where we estimated the storm would hit and then hunkered down, waiting to be deployed. Immediately after the powerfully destructive storm swept across the region, we began our massive relief effort. Large groups of regional disaster relief coordinators gathered in the mornings to receive briefings from the Salvation Army hierarchy. After a few days, the US military finally arrived on scene to assist in the efforts. Our mobile feeding trucks were loaded up with supplies estimated to be sufficient for the tasks and dispatched to various locations throughout the Gulf Coast region. I also packed cases and cases of Bibles, with the intention of giving people some of the wealth God had given me.

Soon after Katrina struck, we loaded my rig with enough supplies to feed about 250 people. I had a crew of volunteers with me, along with my cases of Bibles. We were dispatched to an area of town that was surrounded by destruction. There were gas stations with only skeletal framing left, trees uprooted and set down elsewhere, churches destroyed, and neighborhoods with the remains of homes that looked like piles of match-sticks heaped up all over. Within a few days, there was a stench of rotting flesh in the air. We set up our gear in a parking lot and began offering comfort—sandwiches with bags of chips, fruit cups, refreshing drinks, and the like, along with words of encouragement and personal prayer. Each day I posted a brief paraphrase of some uplifting scripture on a small chalkboard next to the feeding window.

Not a single Bible had been taken by the time we fed some 400 people and ran out of bread, about 1:00 in the afternoon. There were about 100 people in line still waiting to be fed, and it was as hot as the blazing sun outside.

A distinct, creepy, dead silence hung in the air. Not a single bird could be heard. There was no wind. To me, it felt as if a nuclear bomb had just gone off. I thought about how it must have been similar to the eerie days immediately after 9/11 at Ground Zero.

I stood looking out of my food truck window at the devastated, tired, and hungry crowd. I watched the countenance of the survivors go from bad to worse as news of our shortage rolled down the line. Eventually, one of my volunteers said, "You're going to have to go out there and talk to these people or there is going to be a riot!"

I had no idea what to do, but I knew my volunteer was right. I stepped out of the truck and positioned myself on a slight hill above the line of people and about thirty paces away, so that I could address the whole crowd. Pointing to the chalkboard with the day's paraphrased scripture chalked in, I began addressing the crowd in a loud voice, "People! We in America can't complain!" The crowd was beginning to get out of control, and I had to do something.

I continued, pointing to the chalkboard and saying with a loud voice, "Instead of complaining, we need to observe the Word of God!" That day, the words written there were, "Praise and thanksgiving prepares the way of the Lord, so you can see His salvation." I quoted what was written to the crowd and then began to differentiate between praise and thanksgiving.

"Praise is acknowledging who God is and His marvelous attributes," I shouted. I explained that praise to God is admitting that, if nothing else, He allowed this terrible storm to happen. I said that He knows each star by name and holds every single one of them in place, while also perfectly knowing every single hair on each person's head. I told them that not even a sparrow falls from the sky apart from His will, describing that acknowledging this as true is a form of praise to God.

I went on to tell them that giving God thanks is a bit more obvious, "We can thank God that we are alive today to seek Him and experience His goodness. We don't know how many people have died from this tragedy. And we are not them!" I told them of a few other reasons to be thankful.

Then, springing from my private time in the Bible early that morning, I began sharing out of Luke 13. That's just what was there, in my heart.

"There's a place in the Bible where tragedy killed people, and Jesus challenged the crowd by saying, "Do you think they died that way because they were more wicked than you? I tell you, no! But unless you repent, you too will all perish!"

When I had read "all" earlier that morning, it was like a ringing bell in my heart and mind. I emphasized this word to the crowd and began detailing the sins of America.

My past wasn't all that far away so I started there. "Many of us in America are prostitutes for money! Or drugs, or booze! Or whores to our own will!" I continued, "Our country is filled with adulterers! Many of us live large and care only for ourselves while others all around us are suffering terribly!" I told them that idolatry is placing other things before God, and, well, I just gave them a real ration.

This whole open air sermon only took about eight to ten minutes and, frankly, I started to get a little panicky after chewing them out, telling them that we all needed to repent and realizing that I was out of words to say. So, abruptly, I said, "Now, we're gonna pray!"

I lifted my head to the clear blue sky and I lifted both of my arms in the air as I began to loudly pray to God in front of everyone, "Father, we do choose to praise You for Your sovereign control!" I offered heartfelt praise to God, then thanks in front of everyone. Then I said, still looking upward with my arms extended toward the sky, "Father, we have all of this meat and all of these hungry people, but we don't have any bread. Give us bread, Father, so that they may eat, in Jesus' Name!"

I knew I was talking to God, but I still had kind of a sinking feeling, Now what? As I lowered my arms and head, I realized that a cargo van had just pulled up behind me. I turned around to see what the driver wanted.

He jumped out of the van, happy as can be, and said, "I got a van load of gourmet bread. Do you want this bread?" At his words, the crowd freaked out. Most began weeping, many falling to their knees and crying out to God. The line broke and the crowd rushed my cases of Bibles, leaving me without any Bibles in literally less than one minute.

People were approaching me in tears and asking for prayer, giving their lives to Jesus or recommitting themselves to His Lordship. One lady who reported being a registered nurse, approached me and exclaimed through obvious heartfelt tears, "I've been spending my money in the casinos, and I knew I should have been helping the poor!"

Now encouraged by the Holy Spirit's activity, I replied, "And where are those casinos now, ma'am?"

"Gone!" she said, "They are all gone! Jesus, forgive me!"

We began loading the bread from the van into our mobile food truck—delicious bread with a wide variety of crusts, different seeds like poppy or sesame and sprinkled with garlic or other seasonings. Before we finished emptying the cargo van a Salvation Army truck arrived, loaded with more bread. I personally shook hands and prayed with many people that day, and without exception each one I spoke with made a decision to follow Jesus.

That registered nurse came back to serve as a volunteer every day after that, in the blazing hot sun, and with a spring in her step and a smile on her face that could only be described as from God.

As it turned out, back home my family needed bread too.

AT ALL COST

The harvest was plentiful, just as Susan's dream had declared, and we were able to meet and help a lot of people. But by the time of Hurricane Katrina, we were struggling financially. The contrast was so dramatic. We went from having as much money as we wanted in the FAA—always, even if in debt—to relying on the invisible, constantly, to meet our needs.

We recognized God's mercy and provision daily. One gentleman felt God lead him to bless us with a "payment plan" immediately prior to my time with the Salvation Army, and he was faithfully fulfilling his pledge. We also kept receiving sporadic financial gifts and help. Just prior to our daughter Beth's seventh birthday, Susan was browsing through a magazine mailer. A certain massive blow-up water slide caught her eye. It cost hundreds of dollars. She reports thinking, *Lord, I used to be able to just go and buy something like that.* She says she didn't even ask Him for it, but closed the magazine and threw it in the trash, with a sunken heart, thinking that if He's not giving something to us, then she didn't even want to be looking at those things. She didn't mention any of this to anyone. Two or three days later, someone called, "I'm at the mall. I've purchased something for Beth's birthday. Please come and pick it up." Susan drove to the mall. The person opened the back of her SUV to reveal something large, covered with a blanket. When the friend removed the blanket, Susan wept, seeing that exact water slide.

It did seem like we were constantly in need of a financial miracle, and constantly erupting with abandoned praise to God for providing them. So real. So dramatic. And our children were not suffering as vagrants either. They would later decide to give that slide to needy children through the Salvation Army, having enjoyed it for a summer. Someone who doesn't know the intimate details of our journey might see our children as victims. But they don't know about the many times God sent us to Busch Gardens or the multiple times He sent us to Disney World, or nice dinners or sweet birthday parties, all while being "completely broke." Our children have seen God provide our needs over and over, and have felt loved, safe, and secure.

We were getting by, miraculously, even though the Salvation Army salary was not large. Or enough. We had to choose between offering our whole tithe—we had learned this meant giving the first ten percent of all of our income to God—or pay our mortgage payment. We couldn't do both.

We were grateful to have any income and knew that all of our income was from God's kindness to us anyway, so thanking Him with the first and best portion of what He had been providing was very important to both of us. So, overflowing with faith because of the mystical and tangible events going on all around us, we decided to tithe first and trust God for the house payment. In fact, we were pretty darn sure He would just pay off the house altogether so that we could testify to His faithfulness in the matter. We thought, *Everyone will see God pay off our mortgage, and we will have all the more money to help others!* Yet, as the summer unfolded we went one month after another tithing rather than paying the mortgage payment. When Hurricane Katrina struck in August we were significantly behind on our mortgage payments. Something needed to happen.

Susan and I discovered a special way for us to seek God together, especially when the chips were down. We had gone through traditional communion services at church. "The Lord's Supper," the priest would call it, as he served the bread and wine to the congregation. As we matured in our faith, we began to see how personal and powerful this symbolic ceremony is, and we started sharing communion together at home as well. So with our faith-labor at a critical point regarding our finances, we went to the communion table at home. Well, it was our kitchen table and the elements before us were some grape juice and bread. We knelt at the table and poured our hearts out to God for a couple of minutes and then began to be quiet and still, accepting by faith His love which He had demonstrated by giving His life for us.

As we ate the bread and drank the juice, representing the life and salvation that we have through Jesus, we both sensed God speaking to us. I heard the statement, "Your well-being will not be surpassed by another." I first thought, *Is that even in the Bible?* Then I thought, *I'm not in a competition with anyone!* Nevertheless, we were in a stubborn situation, and I wanted to believe that this was God's response to me.

After a day or two I hadn't noticed any Bible verses that would confirm this perception, so I was a little bit hesitant to accept what I had heard as an authentic statement from God. I put the outrageous notion on a shelf in my heart, thinking that if it were God, He would initiate showing me the same thing in His Word.

Sure enough, He did. A few days later I read, "You shall be blessed above all peoples." (Deuteronomy 7:14) I didn't think of myself as any better than the next person, just dearly loved. I was shocked by the statement, but as I continued to read I learned that, from the original text, the verse teaches that all of God's children will be blessed more than, and higher than, any other people on earth. This is for any child of God through Jesus Christ. That was all I needed to whole-heartedly embrace my kitchen communion table experience.

Susan's encounter at the communion table that day was a vision. To clarify, dreams and visions from God are pretty much the same thing. They are spiritual revelations that go way beyond any natural ability to perceive, and they will never contradict God's written Word. In other words, they can't be created or merely imagined by humans. Generally, as in this case with Susan, and like her visit from Jesus at the bank, a vision is a clear spiritual perception received while not sleeping.

I need to point out that not all dreams and visions are spiritual perceptions. Some are just literal junk that's floating around in our souls (mind, will, emotions). Some spiritual perceptions are from God and some are from humanity's enemy, Satan. The results, or "fruit," of dreams and visions will prove or debunk their authenticity; in other words, whether they are actually from God or not. The immediate evidence of spiritual perception from God is peace, or at least help for us to remain submitted to the peace He offers. Someone who is submitted to God and spending time with Him in His Word will be more apt to "see" or "hear" His Spirit no matter where they are, resting or awake and active.

That day while we were taking communion, Susan saw us in the middle of a lovely, fully ripe wheat field, reminiscent of her earlier vision that revealed we were being promoted to the harvest field, although we did not recognize the correlation until years later. The wind was causing a rolling effect across the field, as uniform waves of heads of wheat bowed under the weight of the moving wind. She testified that it produced a powerful sense of peace and well being within her. That positive "fruit" helped serve as authentication.

She said that as she enjoyed the sight, fully enthralled within it, a lightning bolt came out of nowhere and struck nearby, startling her out of the vision. Once again, we saw that God was telling us the fields are ripe (people are ready to hear about Jesus), and that we needed to get to work while we still had time (before God's final judgment, represented by the lightning bolt). The "Jesus is coming!" urgency continued to echo around us.

By late September a foreclosure notice arrived in the mail. We had been tithing and earnestly trusting God to honor His word in that regard; in fact, this is part of what liberated me to work so feverishly, up to twenty hours a day, in those post-Katrina days without being preoccupied with our financial dilemma. So when the foreclosure notice showed up, I had to ask God, "What about this whole tithing thing? What happened to the heavens being opened and blessings being poured out, so much so that we don't have enough room to put it all?" I had read that famous passage of scripture in Malachi 3 and was wondering what went wrong. Either God wasn't telling the truth or this Word wasn't finished having its way with us. I knew and had to accept that sometimes His Word is tested in the heart of a believer, to bring about greater reward—like spiritual blessings so rich you can't contain them all, eventually even leading to greater outward rewards. He's all about drawing us deeper into a healthy and fruitful relationship with Him. And that's where I was.

But while I was questioning God, with His outrageous promises of prosperity and recent mighty acts still fresh in sight, I got to my knees and asked Him for the winning lotto numbers. I was trying to reconcile what I was seeing in the natural (a foreclosure notice) with what I was so sure He was saying (leaps and bounds of progress). "Here's a way You can fulfill Your promises to me, Lord!" And I clearly heard a series of six numbers, too. I was so excited, knowing I had heard from God.

I jotted the "winning numbers" down and rushed to the store. If you're so holy that you've never bought a lotto ticket, I'm sharing that you have to pencil in your numbers within little empty circle-type bubbles. I did that, and to my astonishment the numbers I had heard from God and recorded on the lotto ticket purchase-form created a perfect Christian cross! I just knew I had struck it rich! After days of coming unglued waiting for the lotto drawing so I could go and claim my millions, the day of the drawing finally came. I didn't win cash from the lotto drawing. But I was certainly confronted by the Christian cross that I myself drew on the lotto form, with numbers that I believed I had received from God.

I determined that I didn't win because God had something even better in store for us, but with a fresh and ever sobering view of the cross in sight. Much as I didn't want to face the truth, I knew what God was telling me to do. I had been walking with God, vibrantly, for two years now and this specific trial created a huge confrontation between the many heavenly, blissful realities we had come to know and the stupid mortgage payment. And what was in my face, to resolve the confrontation? A cross. I needed to give up everything, I mean everything, for what was on the other side of that cross.

That meant denying myself the instant gratification I had embraced for most of my life. Instant access to the beach with my board, instant vacations throughout the Caribbean, instant status and luxurious living in New York, even instant answers to the prayers to meet our mortgage. All had to go. In a sort of spiritual inventory, we were hearing, "What would you withhold from Me? Am I here to do what you want Me to? Or are you here to do what I want you to do? Would you give Me that foreclosure notice, and everything associated with it, including the home it is attached to? You can't follow Me with that giant thing on your back. I love you and My extravagant promises are real, awaiting your decision. The ball is in your court."

We could even hear Him laughing with joy, anxiously anticipating His opportunities to bless us. This same message in various forms rang loud and clear for weeks in our home, from Jesus' teaching about passing through an eye of a needle to His declaring that anyone who is not willing to give up all that they have cannot be His student. Everywhere we turned—TV sermons, daily devotionals, Sunday sermons, personal Bible study—the same, harmonious message shone through, "Follow Me!"

I began to clearly see that if I chose to not follow Him, I would make myself responsible to uphold all that we had, meaning a second job and more money to make ends meet. Would I choose to be a slave to maintain my own possessions and desires? Or would I let it go to follow Jesus and live the ultimate thrill? The picture was clear. I had already been a slave to my own desires when I worked for the FAA and that left me not only completely worn out but in a heap of ruins. I was not willing to repeat that scenario with the Son of God, so clearly passing by an opportunity to join Him along His journey. I needed to be like the Bartimaeus I had heard about in church two years earlier. He didn't let Jesus pass by without making sure he was in hot pursuit. By now, the words I heard that Sunday were hard as a rock within me, "and he followed Him." Every confrontation had already been resolved, for me, in those few words. And God gave Susan the grace to agree.

Susan embraced her total inventory before God, as if He held one thing after another before her, "Would you withhold this from Me?" She would respond, "No, Jesus! I would not withhold that from You!" Item by item of our possessions were being released to Him from her heart. For me, it was a wholesale barnburner. All our "stuff" was like trash that was trying to keep me from moving forward with God. It must all go–all of it at once!

In our hearts, God's promises were more real than the foreclosure notice. We just needed to follow Him at all cost for them to be realized. The theme of "at all cost" was echoing in the air and our hearts, working its way into and, eventually, through our actions.

We called a realtor to discuss selling our home on a Friday night. By Sunday, before we even put a for sale sign in the yard, we were in contract to sell the home with a full price offer. It was the highest asking price in our neighborhood, and there was no negotiation. The realtor paid our mortgage in arrears! He was also new in the Lord, and when we called to ask him to list the house, he gladly *offered* to get us caught up on the payments without our even asking him. He was the person who sold us the duplex condo a few years earlier. The only contact we had with him after that was when he invited us to attend his baptism. Other than the baptizer and the realtor, we were the only people in attendance at his ceremony.

All day Saturday, Susan had been concerned about the condition of the house. She began planning to paint this or repair that before we put a sign in the yard, but none of that was necessary. We came out of the transaction, quickly and debt-free, with a little more than $26,000 in our bank account. Before we moved out of the home, we invited neighbors to come and take whatever they wanted. One lady told us, about two years later, that when we allowed her to do that, going through our house to take whatever she wanted, she was astonished and could not let go in her heart and mind such an act of charity. She said that she gave her life to Jesus because of the events of that day.

I gave my two-week notice at the Salvation Army, and in about a six-week period, all that we had was winnowed away. We shed our worldly possessions and all of their associated strings attached—like self-sufficiency and the burden of having to keep all of our stuff by the sweat of our brow. We kept our children, our Jeep and our cell phone. That's it. Well, we also had a few pieces of luggage with some clothes in them.

I'm not telling every reader to do what we did. We're simply saying that there is nothing He could ask us to give up which is worth retaining. Nothing. He's not trying to get stuff from us, but give a better life to us. Also, the point must be made that we weren't doing these things to become righteous before God. Jesus has already done that. This was about our two-year-old love affair with God. We were responding to what Jesus had done, having just begun to taste and see that God is good.

We were so overjoyed to be walking with God that we sowed, sowed, sowed all that we had, including the profits from the sale of our home. We did keep $2,000 "to be reasonable." How would this unfold? We did not know, but we excitedly rushed to Him to see.

A PLACE TO LAND

I sat in a hotel room two or three days after we had left all behind to follow Jesus. I was so geeked-up in His love that I wasn't being threatened by our circumstances, but I was a bit puzzled that we hadn't received all that we had expected by then. In our sold-out state, literally, we fully expected that a new, debt-free home from God would be right there waiting for us on the other side.

I knelt bedside to pray and a phrase leapt out at me, "Our God is an all-consuming fire!" Oh, I get it! I had been expecting some good feeling polish to be put upon our lives. But God knew we needed something different, including some fire-requiring refinement on my part.

In my life as an air traffic controller, I valued my intellect and practicality, and my keen abilities to handle a lot all at once. Yes, I was excited to embark on this new adventure, leaving my old life behind, but what would I do when grim circumstances arose in my path? To follow Jesus would require giving up doubts, giving up cares, giving up worries and desires. It would cost simple, child-like trust.

So, you see, He created faith in us to believe we were

entering into a new and more glorious life with Him, and then instead of greeting us with a new home, He greeted us to refine our faith, with a hearty "Don't doubt! Don't worry! Don't turn back!" His love in our place of need would burn away doubts and more, and would open the way for us to see His love continue to meet our needs, supernaturally and tangibly.

A few days later, it was 9:00 a.m. and we had to be out of our hotel room "by noon tomorrow." Susan and I entered into a fast, a spiritual discipline of denying ourselves food for a time, to express our earnest desire to be in harmony and step with God. At 9:30 a.m. my cell phone rang. It was a friend who explained that he was going out of town for a week, leaving noon tomorrow, and he wanted to know if I could housesit for him. I thought, *Is there food in the fridge?* To this day, I have no idea if he was aware of the actions we had just taken in our lives. As I said, we didn't broadcast our actions all over the place. The people we invited to walk through our home and take what they wanted we had quietly called, after prayer.

I assured my friend that we would be very glad to housesit for him. Susan and I maintained an acute faith for a miraculous rescue from God, a debt-free home of our own. We didn't know how in the world God would do it, but we extended our faith to Him and refused to let go of the hope that He would grant us this one desire of our heart. We continued to seek Him and received amazing dreams, visions and words from the Bible that harmonized with everything we were experiencing. His promises from the Bible were like a solid rock for us to stand upon.

That week came to an end on Saturday and we had to be out of my friend's home by 6:00 that night. I knelt and as I prayed, tears began streaming down my face, "Father, what are we going to do? Don't You see that we are being left out on a limb here? We need Your help. Where is Your help, Lord?" On and on I went, crying and asking questions. Then a statement resounded that halted my inquiries—"Are you quite finished? Now rise up and move forward victoriously!" I could feel His power inspire me to get up off my knees and get moving.

The tears stopped immediately. I rose to my feet and announced to Susan that we would be driving from Florida to Texas to see my father, whom I had not seen in several years. Not for financial help, mind you, or to escape our circumstances either. It just seemed like the right thing to do at the time. She agreed, thinking about the children having time with their grandparents. We gathered our few things and headed to Texas.

During our two-week stay with my dad and stepmom, we shared our faith with them. I suppose, perhaps, prior to that he viewed our steps as unreasonable. My brainiac dad was watching our journey and doing the math. Our steps over the last two years didn't add up—the way I came to get the Salvation Army job; the way our children got Christmas—it was all backwards to him. Either we were crazy, or God was not only real but intimately involved with ensuring we were okay. After being there for two weeks, he saw that the only thing we were full of was love. We were enabled to share great spiritual matters out of God's Word, and my dad gave his life to Jesus.

It was time to return to Florida so our kids could be back for school at the beginning of the new semester. We left Texas on Interstate 10 for the two-day drive back to Jacksonville. We were so uplifted through the time with my parents and the events that took place that we were too busy praising God and thanking Him to think about where exactly we were going to stay. We had no specific destination in mind. It didn't even occur to us until we got much closer to town.

At around 9:00 at night we were about two hours out of Jacksonville, when it dawned on us…Where are we going to stay tonight? We had roughly $200 to our name, that's it. I suggested that we pray. Susan and I held hands as we drove along, "Father, we know You have a place in mind for us to stay. We're asking that You would provide that place now, in Jesus' Name."

In less than a minute I jumped as the cell phone rang. It was a friend I had helped in his return to the Lord about eighteen months earlier. The last time I had seen him was six months before this call, at his wedding. He didn't know anything about our recent faith steps. He called simply to catch up. And we did. Being so full of faith and joy, to God's credit, I did not come across to him as in some sort of desperate need. He was blown away by our actions and asked if he could hang up to speak with his wife and then call me right back. I concurred. We wondered, "Is this You, Lord?"

He called back and generously, amazingly offered for us to come and stay with him and his family. For as long as we wanted.

I replied, "That's very generous of you, brother, but it's late so we are gonna go to a hotel tonight. We will pray about it and get in touch with you tomorrow."

Nearing the absolute bottom of our $2,000, we went to a hotel in Jacksonville that night. And we did pray, but were still unsure if we were to take my friend's offer. The next day, while driving through the parking lot of a grocery store in this city of about a million people, Susan suddenly exclaimed, "Stop!"

I hadn't been paying proper attention, and if it weren't for her shout I would have run into a pedestrian. I slammed on the brakes. To our amazement, the pedestrian was none other than the guy who had called the night before, who had invited us to stay with his family. He rushed to my driver's window, elated to see us, and we all laughed and expressed praise to God at our remarkable meeting. He had been running errands and just happened to stop at this grocery store on his way home. And here we were, laughing together, in person. I'm so glad I didn't hit him with my Jeep.

Everyone agreed that it was God's will for us to be together. This brother and his wife were extremely welcoming and gracious to our family of (at the time) five. I had read in the New Testament many times about the new Christians sharing community, and here we were doing the same thing with eleven people under one roof.

Our hosts offered us their master bedroom. We strongly declined. How could we? They insisted so emphatically that we finally relented, humbly setting up our whole family in the best this blended family had to offer.

They were busting-at-the-seams excited to have us live with them. They immediately invited us to attend church with them, and we were very glad to join them. On our first

Sunday living with this couple, we listened as the pastor preached to a crowd of more than two thousand people. He began speaking of paying honor where honor is due. He went on to share about how it is good and right to offer your master bedroom to esteemed members of the church, should they come to visit you for a while. The four of us looked at one another with our jaws dropped wide open.

God was so perfect in uniting us with this newlywed couple. Before our arrival, each of them had come to a point where they were having second thoughts about their marriage. Newlyweds with six months together, they were facing what seemed to them mountains of obstacles to their peace and unity. And here Susan and I had made it through hell together, happy to share the wisdom and insight that we had gained through our trials. God used us to help turn their giant mountains into little wrinkles that could be quickly ironed out. While God met their need in this regard, He was meeting our need for a roof over our heads.

Still, I wrestled with a certain longing to be able to provide for my own family. Where was that coming from? God was so near; how could I complain? His promises to us continued to reverberate throughout our hearts and even the hearts of this couple. He had given them glimmers of our family's future, and they were certainly inclined to help us get there however they could. Susan and I tenaciously held to the promise of a debt-free home of our own and eagerly looked for God's guidance on the matter.

At one point while living with this sweet couple, my family had a mere $15 to our name. We had been eager for financial relief from God for weeks and were doing all that we could to turn from the pain of that desperation to the rest and peace of believing His promises. We had personally heard from God many great and amazing things regarding provision, but our circumstances were being most obstinate, trying to make us think what we were hearing was not at all true. This produced a hot trial, but God's grace enabled us to trust Him, giving us peace.

I woke one Sunday morning and heard, "Act like it's already happened."

I replied, "Well, Lord, the only thing we are waiting on right now is some flippin' money! So, okay, today with Your help, I will act like it's already happened, that You have blessed us with some cash."

We went to church with the couple again. As the offering plate was being passed, I leaned over to my wife and whispered, "Well, if it's already happened, surely we would toss this measly $15 in the plate." She agreed. We threw all we had into God's offering plate. The church service, with thousands of people, came and went. No miracle.

Throughout the rest of the day we did our best to remain optimistic through trusting God. As evening approached, I chose to return to the same church for a meeting in which the pastor would be sharing about the church's financial state. At one point the pastor was telling the crowd that the church had been turning children away from their children's ministry because they didn't have enough room to put all the kids. They needed about $100,000 to renovate an area large enough.

I sat stewing in the "Act like it's already happened" word and finally couldn't take it anymore and I raised my hand.

The pastor acknowledged me and I said something like, "Hi, I'm new here, but you seem like a man of integrity to me. I pledge a $1,000 toward that 100 grand within a week," and I turned to the crowd, continuing, "Now all we need is 99 more." Within minutes nearly $120,000 had been offered or pledged.

Act like it's already happened. Well, I had already made the pledge. That had certainly happened. Now I needed to act like I had the ability to honor it. Days went by and my wallet remained empty. I didn't even have the $15 anymore. And then, near the end of the week a gift of more than $5,000 arrived at our doorstep! God had sent another sporadic gift our way through one of his obedient followers.

The next Sunday, I sat in the front row, gleefully ready to fulfill my pledge. When the pastor invited me on stage to share, I felt quite nervous when he handed me the microphone, but found comfort when he whispered in my ear, "You can have my microphone any time, brother." Facing thousands of people, I spoke into the mic. "Pastor," I began, "not only do I have the thousand dollars to fulfill my pledge, but I am very glad to be able to bring in an extra tithe of over $500 too."

The crowd erupted with a fervent, rowdy roar of praise, and I felt almost a familiar high as their elation filled the sanctuary and swept through me like a strong breeze. That's when I heard God's quiet voice. "Don't become intoxicated by their praise. It's not for you." Instantly I was "sober" and joined the crowd in praising God. The children's ministry expanded, and I suppose younglings are heaven-bound now because of this amazing move of God's Spirit.

God has continued to move the hearts of people to send us money. Sometimes accompanied by a phone call. Other times, not. Long-forgotten business transactions found us and paid what was owed us. There were people who were not even acquaintances, but who saw us in church and approached us with cash in their hands, saying God told them to give.

We had no idea that during the season of living in the same house, sharing meals, laughter, and life with our newly-wed friends that we were living the biblical principle of being "in the same house, eating and drinking what they provide, for the laborer deserves his wages." (Luke 10:7) I mean, no one said, "Let's do that!" At the time, I wasn't doing anything that I would have deemed worthy of "wages." I was merely following Jesus and making myself available to serve wherever I could. We were willing and mobile, with no idea where God would take us next.

LEARNING TO ASK

While living with the couple, we were invited to come on staff with a large Christian outreach organization. Our role was to be inner-city ministers. It was the first time it dawned on us that we were called by God to be "missionaries." Oh! That makes a whole lot of sense now!

This is the way we'd been living our lives, through prayer and Bible study and serving others as opportunities arose, but hearing the word as a job title brought it all together for us. We had already been walking within the job description. What a pleasant light bulb to have turned on! I mean, all of that wrestling for our provision and housing and all that trusting God may have been a whole lot easier if we had understood that walking with Jesus the specific way we were doing it had a name. It was called being missionaries.

In this new realization I could see that God was granting me the privilege of providing for my family after all, if even by unconventional means. In truth, a caution even, our journey and the way our lifestyle has unfolded has not been conventional at all. Most full time missionaries have a sending church or non-profit organization, or at least a group of people who make sure they are okay. Honestly, the "full time ministry" thing just happened. It unfolded. It appeared. It worked out that way. We didn't know what we were doing, other than being with God and at all cost. I had no formal pastor or evangelist training. I have no bishop training. I have no writing training; in fact, I failed tenth grade English. I truly believe that my weaknesses, which are huge, all the more prove that God has been doing the work, not me. It is His strength and for His glory, not mine.

Meanwhile, sporadic financial gifts continued to arrive for my family. The intermittent offerings began just prior to my accepting the job at the Salvation Army; they continued throughout my tenure there, and their pace remained unchanged. Our "sending church" turned out to be other followers of Jesus who felt led by God to share their resources with us. We never asked people for money. When our cup ran dry, we learned to lift our empty cup to our Heavenly Father, not as beggars, but as excited children who were confident in His love. We didn't have to beg Him to fill it. It was His pleasure, for multiple reasons. It all unfolded so mystically and void of normal avenues. This helped to create the faith we have today. Out of the invisible that which has value is made to be seen.

After much prayer, we agreed to accept the invitation to join the mission organization, submitting to and embracing God's plan as full-fledged missionaries. That's when the financial gifts changed from sporadic to "Wow!" Once on staff, I learned a very important lesson: There are times, following Jesus, that it's okay to ask people for money. God's presence had been so rich upon us, and we had received such a clear revelation of His love for us, that our strict practice was to avoid asking any human for anything. We had a wealthy and living Heavenly Father right there with us. Why ask a mere human?

The missionary organization instructed us to tell as many people as possible about our aspiration to work in the inner city, and then invite them to "send" us through their financial gifts. Since God had placed us with the organization, we knew that the instructions originated from Him. And we saw many, many times when people's prayers were answered when they gave us their financial support. Of course it's not that they were "buying" miracles; God honored their faithfulness and answered their prayers.

One day while I obediently did what my sending agency, the missionary organization, told me to do—go and share your heart and then invite people to be financial partners—I shared my heart with a man who was an aviator. He loved flying, but was borderline illegal to fly due to failing eyesight. He was about to forever lose his joy of taking flight. While we met, I prayed for God to heal his eyes. Within a couple of days, he reported to me that his eyesight had been restored. He was elated and thanking God. He's been a financial supporter of ours ever since.

Another financial supporter, who was an entrepreneur selling high-tech medical devices, saw sizeable growth in his sales after we prayed with him according to what God had placed upon our hearts. He later shared he didn't think what we'd prayed could ever happen. It did happen, and he ended up selling more in the next year than he could have ever imagined. He's the gentleman I mentioned earlier who has been buying Christmas gifts for our children every year.

Many more amazing things like these happened. To be clear, we were not asking people to make offerings to us, but to God through us. God was sending us as missionaries, and when others supported us with their financial gifts, they were actually giving to God. We learned that God had chosen for us to receive their financial acts of worship as part of His bigger plan. And in doing so, "nutrients from heaven" flowed freely within the Body of Christ in the earth, spiritual and natural resources necessary for the Church to be built up, strong in love.

We had learned our lesson to trust God to provide. He is faithful and He will do it. And, sometimes, maybe someone needs to endure the spiritual discipline of giving, or giving more, to please God's Spirit for the good of His Kingdom and for their very own benefit. Maybe someone has been praying, "God, thank You for providing for me. Where may I sow, to thank You?" And maybe these people, or others who God would have to give, need us to come along as an answer to their prayer, as people sent from God. When we are prompted by God rather than our needs or circumstances to ask for support, we should not hesitate, because there is a larger mosaic happening that we know little about. It made us all the more eager to try and persuade people to give to God through us, knowing that their sacrifices would result in blessings flowing to them in return. We also noticed that God is looking to bless people in the business realm. That's an essential part of His Church as well. Again, I'm not saying anyone bought favor with God. Rather, I'm pointing out two-way communications between heaven and earth that caused divine nutrients to flow liberally within the Body of Christ.

While we were with the missionary organization, Susan became pregnant with our fourth child. As she grew larger in her pregnancy, our friends' master bedroom seemed to be growing smaller to our whole family. So one day, I prayed to God, "Father, Your Word says that even a sparrow has a home of its own and the swallow a nest where she may have her young. Look at Susan, Lord, and provide for us, now, a place where we can expand comfortably."

At that, God will testify, our cell phone did immediately ring, again. It was a colleague with our missionary organization. He said that a single middle-aged man wanted to host Christians in his home for a year because he was feeling lonely yet so materially blessed in his large, empty home. He asked if we would be interested in taking the man up on his offer.

That was one offer we did not hesitate to accept. I joyfully agreed. We moved into a spacious and lovely property with the man who had been languishing in loneliness and brought him a holy storm of blissful, non-stop family activity, just a few minutes away from the hospital where Susan would eventually give birth to our fourth child.

When we brought the baby home to this most blessed environment that God had provided for us and placed the little one in his lap, this man who had been longing for the sense of family laughed with a joyous, glowing face of fulfillment. Priceless. We each shared the wealth God had given us with the other, truly enriching one another's lives.

And yet… I had an unresolved grief with God.

We had two small, older vehicles. Both needed extensive repair and were starting to become difficult to drive. Also, with our family of five, each vehicle was packed to the max. Leading up to our fourth child's birth, we had been asking God for a safe vehicle large enough for six. We believed that He said He would be glad to give us a newer, larger vehicle and we rejoiced in that. We wanted it before the baby was born.

So when the baby came in September 2006, and we still only had the two smaller vehicles, I was mad at God. We drove home from the hospital with our new, larger family of six… in two separate vehicles, recruiting a relative to drive one of the cars with three of our now four children in tow. I was fussing with God, "You said [this] and You said [that]!" Yes, I was mad. It hurt my feelings to be "so favored by God" and yet, here, my precious family was made to suffer—a relative term when I think of the orphans and homeless we've tended to over the years, I know, but I was upset. So upset that I couldn't even drive anymore.

I pulled over to pray, with Susan and our new baby in the back seat, and grabbed my Bible. After venting to God, I flopped it open. And the words that my eyes fell upon put me in my place… "Would you condemn Me to justify yourself?" (Job 40:8) It was Job speaking, who didn't understand what God was doing in his life. From there, I chose to praise Him, no matter what. Even while my family of six went to church in two small, older vehicles for a season.

A month later I shared our calling and labor with a new acquaintance. We visited for about an hour, and I invited him to join our support team. He called the next morning, which happened to be my birthday.

"My wife and I have prayed and do believe we've heard from God. We believe He has instructed us to give you a Chevy Tahoe."

I replied, "Wow, it's my birthday!"

"Happy birthday!"

The first Sunday after my birthday, through no effort of our own, the whole church of thousands of people took notice of my birthday present as people streamed out to take a look at God's goodness to us. Leather seats, sunroof, 4-wheel-drive (beach!). It was a birthday present from Him who takes pleasure in giving good gifts to His children. What do you have to do to earn good birthday presents from loving parents? Nothing, I would think. Just being born is good enough, right? Likewise, being born into God's family brings us into a loving Father's good nature, a Dad who enjoys giving good gifts to His kids.

Meanwhile, we were expectant, again, about where we would live.

NEW CORRIDORS

A couple of weeks before our time to be out of this single man's home, we were invited into another home. A friend had purchased a condominium for his mother and had fully furnished it, but now his mother was not interested in living there. He called me out of the blue and asked if my family would like to occupy the condo, which sat on a golf course, for a year. We prayed about his offer and felt as though it was indeed love from heaven for us on earth. The condo had just the right number of place mats at the dinner table for our family of six, a 52-inch big-screen TV (large for 2007) and pleasantly furnished rooms for everyone in the family. And now that we weren't living with someone else, we were able to enjoy the privacy and intimacy of our own family.

In the missionary organization where we served, the first season of a new staff member is dedicated to developing a financial support team. During that purposeful one-year season, while submitting to God-given authority, I grew to be at perfect peace following God through doing what I was told to do by earthly superiors. As an air traffic controller in the FAA, I had not always submitted to authority well.

I did really enjoy the discipline and authority structure of training. Whether in the military or in the FAA, as long as I was in what happened to be strict training, I thrived, actually enjoying being under authority. I flourished within all of the training environments—and then became the law each time I left those conditions. But God helped me with this at the mission organization, manifesting redemption from my conflict with management in the FAA. I also learned to serve God by asking others to sow into His Kingdom. And I learned to sow as well. And sow we did! We sowed obedience to authority. We sowed spiritual treasures. And we sowed life-saving finances everywhere we could. These things were merely tangible expressions of sowing thanks to God for all that we perceived He had done for us and wanted to do.

In keeping with divine purpose, one year is all we would serve with that organization. I believe, for us, the aforementioned substantive lessons were our reasons for being there and, once fulfilled, we perceived God calling us out, into deeper water. Those lessons were: 1) The huge light bulb of "You are missionaries–it's a way of life!" 2) Do what earthly authority tells you to do (a type of redemption). 3) Be at peace with #1 and #2.

Walking within these things caused us to be a tremendous blessing to others, glorifying God. After that year, with more than fifty people sending us financial support monthly, God called us out. We left honorably, with good relationships intact.

When we left the missions team, our confidence in God (His love, kindness and ability) was much greater. Initially, we lost almost all of our "see-able" support, but we weren't moved by that, because we had been built up immensely by seeing such strong support from heaven. That contributed to a new way of life: Live to be a blessing. Don't be concerned about yourselves. God will uphold a life that is following His Spirit and simply looking to be good to others.

We discovered the meaning behind Jesus' words that spoke of us giving up all that we had to place our money where our hearts were—in His Kingdom—first. In the context of that passage (Luke 12:31-34), Jesus said that following His Spirit in this matter would produce inexhaustible treasure in heaven. We learned that our limitless treasure was intimacy with God, something that can provide any manner of earthly wealth. Placing the well-being of His Kingdom before the well-being of our own home was our way of expressing our devotion to Him. The famous theologian, John Wesley, said that he should be considered a thief if even a nickel (England's equivalent, that is) was found in his pocket when he died. He did not leave loads of money to any children when he died, but he did give birth to, leaving behind, a little thing called the Methodist Church. That "child" then produced many more children (denominations), all of whom have harbored countless souls for Jesus!

From the place of understanding that we were exceedingly rich because of God's love, we were quick to give finances that came into our house to others who needed it more than we did. We believed that our relationship with God could, and would, produce whatever type of wealth was necessary. Like Wesley, who aspired to be caught with nothing because he had spent it all on God, we purposed to keep our earthly bank balance near zero continually. Living this way translated into giving away 70 percent of our income during that one year with the mission organization in which we brought in about $100,000.

A bulk of the seventy grand went to missionaries. Our hearts were ablaze with spreading the Good News as far and wide as we could. The Lord also provided a needy person here and a needy inner city family there; it was our joy to help, being rich in faith, and we always did it prayerfully. We once had the honor of paying to help set up a rental home for a homeless family who had several children and whose dad was an Iraq war veteran. We have discovered that God is very pleased when we put His Kingdom and His cause first in our finances. We have also found that by placing others first the perpetual flow of God's life-giving love truly does seek us out and overtake us.

We didn't have a mortgage at the time, or a car payment, so 30 percent for our family's necessities was sufficient. And of course we sowed the two older cars. We had what others needed and love made it easy and fun for us to give to them, fulfilling their need. It's one thing to be broke because of self-indulgence. It's an entirely different thing to have zero money because you took care of inner city people before taking care of your own family, or because you fed orphans or gave to other missionaries before spending on yourself. The giving with abandonment seemed to prime the pump of God's generosity toward us. I'm not saying you can manipulate God. I'm sharing how we lived. It was very difficult at times and required an abiding, audacious faith, a faith created by Jesus. He called us to this lifestyle and He taught us to give without fear, knowing and relying on His love. I'm not claiming we did everything perfectly, but God's grace was exceedingly rich toward us.

One time Susan was upset with me because we had been giving so much away and our kitchen was absolutely bare. She had tears streaming down her face as she told me about how it wasn't right. In all boldness, to God's glory, I said, "You know what? You're correct. It's not right!" I took her by the hand and led her to the refrigerator. I opened the empty refrigerator, holding its door with one hand, and held an open Bible in my other hand, saying, "Only one of these two things are telling us the truth."

She resolved the conflict by calling on the written promises of God, such as, "Because our God richly provides everything for our enjoyment…." (1 Tim. 6:17)—and we gave Him glory for being so good to us. Then, together, we turned away from what we didn't have to enjoy what we did have, like good health, each other, and the most wonderful children on earth.

Later that day someone called. "God put it on our hearts to take you to a wholesale club for groceries. And do you need gas in your truck?"

This type of thing, confronting circumstances that contradict the truths of God's Word by accepting and boldly declaring His Word, was not a one-time occurrence. It has become our way of life.

Within two months of leaving the missionary outfit and having surrendered all of our supporters to God, we only had about a half dozen financial supporters who had chosen to stick with us. This is when the Spirit of God developed another heartfelt declaration that spilled out of our mouths daily, "You choose the who it's through!" God can work through all people—the homeless, millionaires, or anybody in between. This deep-down belief super-liberated us from being needy before men and helped to empower us to simply trust God, seeing all people equally.

During our closing months at the golf course condo, I began to recognize that I was becoming heartsick regarding having a debt-free home of our own. We had left a mortgage behind and were in faith for a debt-free home, doing all we knew to do to abide in Christ through obedience. We had received a promise from God early in our journey that He would give us a home that would be better than one we could obtain on our own by debt or saving up. Once that was in our hearts, as sure and real, we weren't saving up for a home as little-bits were being provided, rather we used that provision to thank God in advance for the home He had promised. We had kept the faith and yet, after nearly three years, no mighty home-settling rescue had come.

One night through heartsick bedtime prayers I said, "Father, my soul is wounded within me. Where's our stuff? Thank You for answering." That's all I could muster.

The next morning I woke from a dream in which mercy and faithfulness were dispensed to me in pill bottles from a pharmacy. I had told God that I was hurting and He had responded, saying, "I give you just what the Doctor ordered." My daily devotional that morning confirmed the orders, as it asserted in my reading, "I will sing of the *mercies* of the LORD forever; with my mouth I will make known thy *faithfulness* to all generations." (Psalm 89:1, KJV, italics mine for emphasis)

The following forty days became an open corridor in the sky, a highway of holiness into my life that produced an astonishing inner work. First, God showed me that there are times and seasons to let go of our desires, even if it's something God said He wanted to give us. I was instructed to give God a "blank slate" when I came to Him in prayer. In other words, let Him set the agenda.

The message was firm and clear. I concurred and let go of my desire for a debt-free home. Susan stood right there by my side, fully convinced that we should release that long-desired promise back to God. We placed our confidence in God's rich mercy and faithfulness to take care of us His way. Bill Bright, founder of Campus Crusade for Christ, never owned a home of his own after coming to Christ, but lived in very nice homes throughout his spiritual pilgrimage on the earth. That's what God provided him, and he was good with that. His example helped us to be content with God's plan for our lives.

I turned forty years old within this amazing forty-day timeframe of inner work. When I was a teenager, I found the motion, beauty, power and form of the ocean waves to be so alluring that I experienced an irresistible draw toward them. Now, beginning on the eve of my fortieth birthday, after I had gone to bed, I discovered that I had been translated from being drawn by those waves to being captured within living and powerful waves of Mercy and Truth, nuances of perfection, divine attributes. This could be likened to an out-of-body experience. All. Night. Long. My physical body was the shore but the entirety of the rest of my being was one with God while massive waves of Mercy and Truth were ebbing and flowing, washing upon the shore. Now I wasn't seeking to ride ocean waves for a thrill, but I had truly found fulfillment being within these holy moves of perfection, beauty and power. Words couldn't possibly relay the bliss of what I experienced that night. As I "came to" on the morning of my birthday, I heard, "A kiss to My ambassador" and then I lay there in all-encompassing quietness and utter awe for quite a while. I don't claim to be any more special than the next child of God, and I don't mind sharing this amazing kiss from my King either. Sure enough, my subsequent time in the Word that morning produced Psalm 85:10, "Mercy and truth are met together; righteousness and peace have kissed each other." (KJV) Not that I went looking for a passage to justify my perceptions; it's just the way my Bible study happened to unfold–again. I later learned that some versions of the Bible even use the word "faithfulness" instead of "truth" in Psalm 85:10, as my pharmacy dream asserted.

The most critical inner work during this forty-day period shook my soul and altered the direction of our lives. First, God showed me a city on a hill that had suffered a terrible, sweeping power outage. The entire city sat in utter darkness, broken and ruined. It was a heartbreaking, dreadful sight that caused me to panic.

What does this mean, Lord?

My insides churned at the poignant scene. I could feel such intense emotions, not unlike those I suffered in New York at the collapse of the World Trade Center. Could it be this scene was connected to 9/11 and the disasters of that day somehow? Did it represent the brokenness of my life, the loss of my FAA dream? No, I sensed. This was different and it was for now. Then the acute and pointed realization hit me and I cried out, "No! Please, God, no!" I wept as I recognized the darkened city was the Church, at large, in America. It had been torn down and it lay in utter ruins, powerless.

Then I heard, "His power, your gift." Just like the crumbled city, my life had been torn down and lay in ruins. God had given me the extraordinary ability to manage many airplanes in the sky, directing them through invisible corridors. I had the gift to see and maintain pathways and routes coming and going across the sky, allowing the aircraft to reach their destinations without colliding in mid-air. But when I didn't surrender to God's power to hold me up, my life came crashing down and my gift with it. And now. Now I could see that God was renewing my gift through His power. Now he had given me the ability to see and comprehend new things, miraculous and mysterious, visions and dreams, and to hear specific messages from Him. For the benefit of others and definitely not in my own power, my new assignment was being revealed.

At the end of the forty days, the inner work season concluded when, waking one morning, I saw a vision. It was that blank slate I had given God, except now there was a single word written upon it.

Build.

It was a command from God, His agenda. And I accepted, by faith, everything necessary to get the job done, as released to me within His command. The Bible says that where there is no vision the people perish (Prov. 29:18). The word "vision," in the original text, means a sight, dream, revelation or oracle. We had been learning to live this way, for God's glory and the restoration of His Church. I realize there are good, healthy and glowing congregations in America. But, overall, according to the revelation of the darkened city, and its "fruit" plainly seen by the natural eye, the American Church is lacking.

Time to start building.

TAKING FLIGHT

With only a month to go before we needed to vacate the cushy condo, I knelt before God and asked, "What are we going to do? Where are we going to go?" I spent time in prayer, trying to discipline myself by bringing my thoughts, feelings and beliefs into alignment with the many good things God had said to us, so that I could enjoy the peace I knew He wanted me to have.

Suddenly, I heard God laugh. A great big, deep and hearty laugh. My initial response was, "I don't see anything funny here, Lord." That's the day He showed me that the only time we find God laughing in scripture is when the enemy is actively being dealt with. At all their threats and intimidation, He only mocks them and laughs…right before He sends lightning bolts their way to scatter them in terror. Indeed, God was actively working on our behalf and we had found great peace, empowering us to trust Him.

As early 2008 came around, we received two invitations to move in with folks, one of them from my mom. This didn't seem like progress to me, but now I had let go of the desire for a debt-free home of our own. Mind you, God didn't say we couldn't or wouldn't have that. He said, in essence, "For now, forget about it. When we meet, come to me with a blank slate, ready to be written upon, not full of requests or points for prayer. Be ready to listen and take notes."

God made it clear that He was directing us to make the harder choice of moving in with my mother. She loved us dearly and wanted to help us however she could for the cause of Christ. Plus it would be wonderful for her and our children to have this time together. I had nothing against my mother; it was my ego that was pitching a fit. This is where God's heart to minister was born in us. Previously, we were all about following Jesus no matter what. Yes, this did include putting others before ourselves, but now, in preparation for what lay ahead of us, God was taking us lower, lower, lower in humility.

My mother had also grown sensitive to the leading of God's Spirit, so she did not become our bank account. She found the grace to trust God with us and she personally witnessed Him (rather than her) providing our family's necessities. No longer under the instruction of the missionary organization to always ask people for money, I sought God for insight—when to go and ask versus when to be still and wait—and in the meantime I did what was being revealed to me through His Word.

This unfolded with God directing, "Forget about yourself and go be a blessing. I will take care of your needs." He called me to be a blessing by going into maximum security prisons to minister the Gospel, and also volunteering as a court-appointed child advocate as a Guardian Ad Litem in Florida. I served as "the eyes and ears of the judge," visiting the homes of reportedly abused or neglected children. Both of these areas of service turned out to be extremely powerful.

In prison, I saw murderers and rapists and all manner of rough people change. One time, while the story of the Prodigal Son was being preached in maximum security prison, I saw a thick cloud develop at the top of the room, and it grew downward until everyone in the room was sitting within this mystical cloud. The hard, hard faces which entered the room with looks of hate and death began to change, streaming with tears as their hands went up in praise to God. Many were saved.

Another time, I was assigned the specific name of a fellow to pray for before I went in, without any details to his plight. I prayed for him for about two months before I met him. When I met him I was surprised to immediately observe he was blatantly homosexual. Even after all that prayer, I was not prepared for his flaunting demeanor. I chose to love him as though he were perfect, in light of how God loves me, thinking, Jesus made me perfect even while I'm a work in progress. If I really believe that, I will extend the same to this young man. I spent four days with him and never told him that homosexuality is not God's intention for mankind. On the third day, he came to me and confessed his homosexual behavior as sin, declaring that he knew it wasn't right. His confession was like the nurse who had admitted her sin during the Hurricane Katrina ministry. It was a deep down "knowing" that they had been choosing to ignore for the sake of their own pleasures. The man abandoned that lifestyle and gave his life to Jesus. I would return to that prison at least once a month for discipleship, and I myself saw this man and many others grow in their faith.

I sensed God prompting me to service in the area of abandoned children numerous times over several months. I was hesitant, resisting Him, believing that it would be more than I could bear to see specific cases of child abuse or neglect. But God's Spirit was persistent and He refused to allow me to turn my head the other way. I relented, and I was right. It was more than I could bear.

He calls us to roll the weight over and onto Him, and it takes time in prayer for this. For instance, in one case, a child developed physical deformities from being made to lie down, all day every day for years. His head was not round like a grapefruit or a cantaloupe, but nearly completely flat like a ball with very little air in it; it was pancaked. His body had no muscular development either, so he couldn't get himself out of a lying-down position. He was four years old; sweet, innocent, neglected, abused. Case after case broke my heart terribly and God used this to have me cry out in prayer for the whole nation, from depths that I had not been aware were within me. What kind of society produces people who would do such things to innocent children? The same kind of nation that produces wild air traffic controllers, rampant division, mass-murders, greed and gluttony, adultery and so on—basically, all-out selfishness. There are many precious, God-honoring, effective congregations of believers in America. But, clearly, they're not enough.

Between the prison ministry and the child advocate visits, I spent much time in tears, praying for our nation's healing. God upheld my family and provided whatever we needed so these holy tasks could be accomplished without any hindrance—food, shelter, clothing and even family entertainment—so we could just be a blessing.

I began to receive a smattering of invitations to preach in churches on Sunday mornings or at Christian conferences. I'd get one, or two, about every other month. Sometimes people would cheer at the words I shared, other times people would approach me and talk about things that seemed completely irrelevant to anything that had just happened. I purposed to listen to them, although sometimes it was trying. I would always seek God for a debrief, His point of view and counsel regarding each opportunity He had given me to speak publicly. This is a time of sober review for the purpose of future improvement, exactly like the debriefs I would endure after every single training session as an air traffic controller on my way to journeyman status.

I'd pray, "I felt like it went [this way], Father. That guy said it went [that way]. The crowd seemed to think it went like [that]. But what do You say?" He was brutally honest with me, of course, even while being so very tender, loving and assuring.

"Well, if it were a basketball game, son, not only did you miss the hoop, the ball didn't even hit the backboard," He specifically revealed to me on one occasion. And as I recall, that was a message in which the crowd cheered. On another occasion, using baseball, "That was a *foul* ball! But this is all part of the process, so don't be discouraged. It is I, the LORD, who have called you to preach My words, and I will not stop opening doors for you to continue developing your skill. Keep in mind, intimacy with Me will always outweigh your ability to do what I've commissioned you to do. Through your reverent relationship with Me, I will bring much good to you and them, even if you strike out in your preaching."

And there were other occasions of debrief that thrilled me. One time, after a not-so-remarkable delivery, I was shown that I had just hit a grand-slam homerun. Another time, I was the winning jockey in a horse race. After that delivery a man out of the crowd approached me and said, "Good message. You are bold. You know, John the Baptist was faithful, and he got beheaded." Geez. I would always seek God before speaking and be sure to spend adequate time with Him to hear the words He wanted me to share.

God wasn't looking to oppress me, only refine the delivery. He provided ample inspiration to continue in the process of public speaking. I had no problem discerning what God was saying, but there are a myriad of things any minister must work through to get it right in relaying God's message. One famous minister said she died a thousand deaths each time before giving any message publicly. That's true work. Makes a fella glad to remember that God's Word says He even spoke through a donkey.

Then, one Sunday morning when my family and I sat in the pew at a glorious church service with thousands of people in attendance, as I enjoyed some of the finest wisdom I've ever heard flowing from a pulpit, the Spirit of God spoke to me, saying, "Fully two-thirds of the people here today should be out on the streets right now, sharing my love to heal this sick nation. There are spiritual gluttons all over the place in here!" God wasn't telling me that going to church was wrong, or being well fed through a fine pastor was wrong. But He was saying that there was an imbalance at large in the American Church and that this was a root to our society's ailments. I realized I was part of the fat two-thirds in church that morning. Over the next two months, Susan and I became convinced that we needed to withdraw ourselves from the church we enjoyed and go to be the Church, on the streets.

We prayed for God to dispatch us, to show us where the needs were that He wanted us to address. Before long we were impressed to visit the homeless people at the Jacksonville Beaches. We began by regularly bringing bagged lunches to them, with warm smiles and heartfelt words of love and encouragement, not so much telling them that Jesus was the only way to peace, but showing them His love through our steps. I reached out to different churches to see if there were any gaps in coverage regarding caring for the homeless at the Jacksonville Beaches. Sure enough, the only time that the Church was not providing emergency relief to these people was on Sunday morning.

While I continued to minister in prison and serving as a children's advocate in court, this became our church service and our homeless people became our beloved congregation. We developed mutual love and respect for one another. It was so obvious that they rejoiced at our coming; the affection was mutual. They knew and planned for our arrival. We would always prepare to go too, praying together as a family and spending days getting ready for Sunday morning's labor of love.

Our four children gladly drew or colored on the brown paper lunch bags—rainbows, crosses, smiles and such, and handed out these love offerings directly to the homeless. I began gathering blankets or other available resources from all over town. By now, I had relationships with many different churches and Christian organizations in our area. God's Spirit trained us to look for doors of opportunity in conversation to share the Gospel. Many were saved.

We would stroll up and down the boardwalk, offering refreshments and God's love to the homeless. Sometimes, beach-goer strangers would approach us in amazement, "What church are you from? What you are doing is amazing!" People would even randomly come up to me and place cash in my hand through a discreet handshake. Many, many times this was God meeting us at "church" as we routinely spent our last pennies to bring these refreshments. There were times we only had enough gas for one leg of our journey to get to church on the beach. Yet, we never had to ask, beg or borrow to get home safely.

I thought it so ironic, and tragic, that some of these homeless people would forever enjoy their home in heaven while a vast majority of plump Americans with large and luxurious homes were the real homeless ones who would suffer apart from heaven forever. This crushed my heart and I burned to find a way to convince them, too, of this urgent paradoxical truth.

ENDS OF THE EARTH

My mother-in-law in Louisiana met a family at a garage sale and learned that they were leaving everything behind, literally and physically, to follow Jesus. She shared our journey with them and gave them our phone number. We began ministering to them via phone and the internet. Unbeknownst to us, the father of that family started reporting to his relatives in North Dakota that he was receiving amazing, life-altering truths from a fellow in Florida–me.

A major change was at hand.

Meanwhile, Susan and I were experiencing signs that would indicate we were going to be moving. A giant Dairy Queen sign in a dream inspired thoughts of *Great! A land flowing with milk and honey! A sweet land of delicious treats.* Another vision revealed that we were indeed leaving Florida, but would need to get cold-weather coats. We had no idea this brother we were ministering to in Louisiana was giving life progress reports to his relatives in North Dakota. We were just being awed by the clear guidance we were receiving from God and responding by expressing our willingness and gratitude to Him. For two solid weeks, day in and day out, everywhere we turned, every spiritual perception and every biblical word that surrounded us was speaking the same, harmonious message, as if we had hit an oil gusher of revelation.

Ever since we decided to leave everything and follow Jesus, we had been telling Him, "We love You, Lord, and will follow You anywhere, because You love us so! We will go to the Yukon with You if that's what You want!" I don't know where we came up with the Yukon, but it symbolized the ends of the earth to us, and that was our heartfelt expression. Right at the end of this amazing two-week period, I was sitting on the couch one evening with my open Bible in my lap. I had been reading Isaiah 41:9 when the phone rang:

I took you from the ends of the earth, from its farthest corners I called you. I said, 'You are my servant'; I have chosen you and have not rejected you. (NIV)

The person who called was from North Dakota, and I considered that the call may be a heavenly echo of the same verse I was reading on earth. She shared that they had heard about our ministry through the man in Louisiana and asked if we would consider pastoring a small church out in the country. I thanked them for calling and told them we would pray about it.

Susan and I were shocked by this phone call in light of what we had been seeing from the Lord, the heavy coats and all. Still, we purposed to seek God about the call. Looking back, it seems silly to have prayed anymore about it. But it was a big step, and there have certainly been times when we considered that the enemy of God also makes attractive offers to sidetrack the children of God from their true path.

Over the next many months we had a few phone calls with a couple of different people in North Dakota. I also visited the area on a weekend scouting excursion and met with the potential congregation. They advised me that they were too small to care for our family's financial needs. I was not at all daunted by this, responding to them by sharing my belief that if it was in fact God's calling, He would pay for it. They offered to cover the rental expenses of an available farmhouse and seemed hesitantly agreeable to my faith regarding God being perfectly capable to care for my family just fine. I think their hesitation was related to feeling a love-obligation to care for us.

The most intense electrical storm that I've ever seen took place the night before I left North Dakota to return home to Florida during that weekend scouting visit. All night long it looked as though a war, with numerous and varying types of explosions, was taking place overhead as lightning continually raced through the night in any and every direction. The constant flashes were so brilliant that, when I did drift off to sleep, I was awakened by them. I've never seen anything like it, even after living in North Dakota for nearly seven years now and growing up in Florida, the lightning capital of America.

I got to my knees the next morning, the morning I was to return to Florida from North Dakota, as I normally would upon rising from bed. I'd normally hear some edifying song during prayer or some Bible verse would pop straight to mind (that, often, would then appear in my routine Bible study) or some other spiritual caress would most often greet my morning bowing before God, as He is always so gracious to welcome me into another day with Him.

This morning, however, I was assaulted. That had never happened to me before. It was as if there was a real heavenly battle going on, and I somehow got caught behind enemy lines on earth! I heard evil threats and shocking accusations, (that I will soften for this text): "Who do you think you are? Your destruction has come!" I had just witnessed an amazing display of hostilities in the natural through the powerful lightning storm and was now assaulted from the spiritual atmosphere as well. Again, as if behind enemy lines. The evil enemy who was responsible for the horror of 9/11 stormed against me, spewing hatred and lies in an attempt to destroy any possibility of building up God's kingdom in North Dakota.

Okay, I thought, *There's serious work to be done here. Duly noted.*

I returned to Florida and we continued our way of life—prison, children's advocacy, homeless—while seeking God about the possibility of a move to take on the battle and demonstrate Christ's victory in North Dakota. Our attitude was victory to the uttermost. That's not to say we haven't had the snot beat out of us on occasion! But, frankly, victory was so formed in us that we gave little weight to the taunts I had heard. We acknowledged them as real, but immediately began stripping them of their wow-power through turning our gaze upon what Jesus did on the Cross.

About two months later I received clear guidance that it was time to pack our bags. Susan sought God for herself and then began packing our household for a move while I went into prayer for the necessary finances regarding this task. Within three days we had received the finances we would need to move our family to North Dakota, about $5,000 in all. Without any concerted fund-raiser, our bank account went from less than $100 to all that we needed to move from Florida to North Dakota.

As we drove past The Gateway Arch in St. Louis, the "Doorway to the West," we were elated to go through this door, in a sense. It was Labor Day 2009, and we drove with the prospect of our new work right in front us. For days after that we drove through mature corn and then fully ripe wheat fields. This brought us so much excitement as we considered these things in light of spiritual matters, including Susan's vision years earlier of being in a ripe wheat field. We overflowed with His promises and thereby hope, joy, and excitement.

It was late in the evening on September 10, 2009, when we arrived at our farmhouse clear out in the middle of nowhere, with the nearest Walmart Supercenter a distant ninety minutes away. The home had been prepared by our new, small, loving, receiving congregation for our arrival. Our new abode was literally in the middle of a vast, ripe wheat field.

Without any intentional planning, our first full day in North Dakota was September 11, 2009, exactly eight years to the day from the horror of 9/11. The number eight, biblically, represents new beginnings. This was our first day in a new land with a new church. That first day, as we drove to see the church where we would be working, we found ourselves on a long, straight, narrow, and perfectly level road through nothing but wide-open, ripe wheat fields. Directly in front of us was a rainbow that looked as though its pot of gold rested directly on our path ahead. In our rear-view side mirrors, Susan and I both rejoiced at seeing the darkest and most furious looking storm clouds behind us. We thought, *All of our troubles are behind us! Glory is right there, straight ahead!*

Our pastoring in a small, isolated town of North Dakota about twenty-five miles from the Canadian border started out well enough. In fact, we all celebrated together, the small, loving congregation and us, and the word-picture of being on a long, narrow, straight, level road with rich promises ahead and storms behind was an apt sight. We were along the way, in transition as it were, on that long road forward.

For the next twelve months I got to cut my teeth on preaching from the pulpit every Sunday morning. I had no formal training, was in a new land with people I didn't know and felt very, very inadequate. I feel a great deal of compassion for the weekly listeners back then. Even so, the strength of God empowered and encouraged me every time I stood in the pulpit to deliver His Word.

True to His mercy and faithfulness, God provided finances for my family just fine; most came from outside of the congregation. In fact, this supernatural provision probably preached to the congregation much more effectively than my mouth did. The church people were impressed by God, by the way He so faithfully cared for me and my family. His love was made apparent to them in that here God was sending money from all over the nation so that they could have a pastor. There were many comments to me from the small congregation about the extraordinary provision we enjoyed, at a time in our journey in which we saw the intimate provision of God as more of a given than something out of the ordinary. The extraordinary had become quite ordinary to my family in this matter.

The faith we had learned to draw upon for our inner family life and its needs was now being exercised outwardly, in the realm of outreach. We were turning our faith-muscles away from our own needs to using that exact same faith-energy to feed others spiritually, in a progression that was obvious to us through following Jesus.

Before long, out of laboring to be still and quiet, trying to find God's *best* activities for me in a new place rather than just the good, I found my way to visiting elderly homes to get to know the treasures there and conduct Bible studies with them, and I also found my way to a small jail that was just over an hour from our home, to minister there. Plus, a homeless ministry from our church was born and travelled to the nearest city to share the love of God. I believe that loving congregation was meant to get us to North Dakota, for the subsequent labor of church planting. "Build," God said.

At the end of our first year, I resigned from serving our little country congregation. When fundamental differences arose regarding church polity, we all recognized, together, that our time had been good but not meant to last. Their pulpit had been a transition for me. One saint suggested that it was as if they were like the solid rocket-fuel boosters of the Space Shuttle, designed to get me off of the ground and into another place. Mind you, those boosters are not disposable but invaluable for the task at hand, a must for the mission, and reusable. May that congregation always be a blessing for Jesus and may He be pleased to bless them for their service.

A few people left the congregation to be with Susan and me, and we began conducting home meetings three times a week to wait upon the Lord quietly, while we carried on the aforementioned outreaches we'd begun after moving to North Dakota. Over three months of meeting this way, three times a week, a word-picture of fresh ministry did surface, even the name, Bethesda (meaning, House of Mercy or House of Grace). Then as I woke one morning, the Spirit of God spoke to me, saying that He had work for me to do in Michigan. I replied, "Michigan? We just got to North Dakota, Lord." About a half hour later, I was writing down my perception, and it occurred to me, "Oh, Michigan City, ND. That's less than an hour away!"

During the middle of the week I went to scout the town and noted a small community church. Susan and I set out to quietly attend one of their services, to see what God would do. We did not go to tell them that we were sent by God to minister. When we arrived at their posted service time on Sunday morning, the doors were locked and we were the only ones there.

A few days later, after prayer, I called the contact number for the church and the lady who answered was elated to receive my call, saying, "We were just crying out to God about what to do with the building!" She shared that they had not been having any services or meetings there for years, that the building had been sitting vacant. Then I told her about my perception of God's voice, to work in Michigan (the way locals refer to Michigan City), and we agreed to meet and pray together.

Turns out, my North Dakota mission was to work with

God to plant a heavenly outpost behind enemy lines. We were building a church to strategically oppose the enemy who had assaulted me before we moved to North Dakota. The church, a place where God is at home and a Christ-centered environment, is established on earth as it is in heaven. It is interesting how when we were called to minister to the homeless at Jacksonville Beach, the same kind of mystical "I have prepared a place for you" arose. There, a Sunday morning opening. Here in North Dakota, all the food, shelter, clothing, family entertainment we needed was provided—and a physical building to settle in and serve within as well.

Around the same time frame that we began ministering in Michigan, ND, God provided us a lovely home on three acres just a few miles from our original farmhouse. We've rented that home, paying a widow's remaining house payments. All the while, half or more of our financial support flowed to us from other than the small congregation that we tended. Receiving financial support in this way worked to confirm the call, encouraging us and those we served that this was a "God thing" and not just some charismatic guy upholding his own desire by his own efforts. Right after our five-year anniversary of worshipping God there, the owners of the church building gifted the building with its grounds to us.

Over the years of our following Jesus, I ended up turning down three separate opportunities to attend different seminaries. One was a full scholarship, including housing and provision for my family. When I sought God for each, I believe He said in essence, "I would bless you through that, but there is another way, and it will give greater glory to My Name." I turned down the seminary opportunities in faith for greater glory to His Name.

He had shown me that many educated people place their confidence in their education, a type of armor, at the cost of discarding Him as their shield, and that I could be part of His correction in this matter. If I were willing to be weak, meaning having no endorsement from this or that accredited organization, His strength could shine through me. Talk about weak? We had no missionary organization backing us up. No sending-church backing us up. No organized natural assistance whatsoever. Only Jesus and those He tapped on the shoulder on our behalf. And that, only "along the way." The apostle Paul said he boasted in his weaknesses because he knew they meant the power of Christ rested upon him. Likewise, God's grace, His approval when we didn't deserve it, empowered us to embrace many weaknesses for His glory.

Years later, I was invited to a pastor's retreat for a certain denomination. Hundreds of pastors were in attendance, and word got around about the pastor who was not part of the denomination. I was creating curiosity, I suppose. There was a swirl of interest about me and "my steps." When one of their most successful pastors asked me if I was bi-vocational I had no idea what he was talking about and replied, "Bi-what?" After selling our home to follow Jesus, the notion that God would pay for His will for me to preach was so real to me that it never even occurred to me that I might have to work to support my family while carrying out God's will for my life. He's the One who commanded me to raise a reverent family. Would He not richly provide *everything* necessary to do it? He has. Most of these pastors were working full time jobs while in full time pastoral positions. I'm not saying

I was (or am) any better than anyone else, but that there's a different way than what is normal within that denomination and with a large portion of pastors in America. I don't mind being considered "ordinary, uneducated people," (Acts 4:13), while bearing authentic fruit that proves we are with the Living God.

INTO ANY WILDERNESS

It was only after we got to North Dakota that we came to realize the vivid connection to Dairy Queen's "The Home of the Blizzard." North Dakota has a long, harsh winter season, a far cry from my beloved sandy beaches and warm, sunny days. Winter is for introspection, a time to stay inside, not step out into the 50-degree below zero, harsh and deadly blizzard.

John the Baptist, the rare breed with whom I related as an air traffic controller, and whom, I had been reminded, was also beheaded, spent much time in the wilderness too. I liken the frigid and dangerous blizzard spiritual environment we have endured to John's time in the wilderness. From my Quest Study Bible regarding John the Baptist, "The harsh climate may have helped to focus his attention on God. Being separated from the economic and political powers of his day allowed him to speak his words of judgment more freely. His chosen lifestyle also clearly distinguished him from other religious leaders who enjoyed living near the halls of power." John's time in isolation worked like a forger's fire to make him a hard instrument, another facet of being in God, separate from but equally as real and important as the soft, nurturing mother (Dairy Queen) facet of God.

God can turn any wilderness, any harsh environment, into a place of blessing. Even healthy trees don't look very fruitful in the winter, but their appearance changes in the spring. My wife and marriage were pulled out of scorched territory and are now truly blissful. Our four children, (spanning from ages nine to eighteen), have not succumbed to the perilous influences of pop culture. To God's credit, our entire family is wholesome and personally reliant upon Jesus.

This is a major point of Christianity, that through having Christ-centered lives, believers can see any harsh circumstance produce a peaceful abode. I recall some of those men in maximum-security prison, believers whose faces emanated peaceful, joyous light in a dark place. As we have given our all to follow Jesus, we've enjoyed tremendous peace, security and personal abundance. This nation's security is directly related to its individual citizens' worship.

The home of the blizzard, this frigid and tough environment where we live, is in the geographic heart of North America and known for a general sense of wholesomeness. These are some of America's best folks. Ask any native North Dakotan and they will quickly tell you that they are a hardworking people. For generations they have worked hard. Very hard. They have needed to be self-sufficient to a large degree in order to survive.

Hard work is fine, unless it is being done out of order. Jesus said to seek His kingdom and His righteousness first. No one knew this better than I did. I was self-sufficient as an air traffic controller, relying on my own strength, and when testing came, I collapsed.

This attitude of self-sufficiency is magnified and made worse when it's translated into spiritual matters. At the point that someone's work becomes what they believe makes them right before God, at that point, they have escalated beyond any measure of healthy self-sufficiency to self-righteous. I mean, for instance, when people go to church regularly and consider themselves to be pleasing to God because of what they have done, they are opening the way for the enemy.

Over and over, various Christians would tell me, "There's a hard, hard spirit of religion in this area." What is the giant called a spirit of religion? It is a real and ferocious spiritual entity of darkness that settles in any place that will facilitate it. It comes to steal, kill and destroy all that is pleasing to God, just as the evil entity came to me and Susan in our bedroom all those years before and tried to destroy our marriage. The evil spirit of religion is facilitated through human attitudes of self-sufficiency, that is, relying on one's own strength rather than relying on God's.

America's self-sufficient heart has grown sick before God.

The people of Jesus' day asked Him what works they must do to please God. Jesus gave exactly one answer: Believe in the One He sent (John 6:27-29). Of course, we all need God's gracious Spirit to work on us so we can believe and respond appropriately. If I had admitted my own self-sufficiency and surrendered my all to Jesus before 9/11, I think I would still be an air traffic controller today. But I tried to hang onto my life my own way. Jesus promises that is how you lose your life and says that if you give up your life for His sake, He will save it. (Matthew 16:25)

The week that I turned seven years old in Christ, in October 2010, I had an encounter with God that left me trembling for days, and helped prepare me to begin the church-plant in Michigan City over the next six weeks. We had been walking in nothing less than the miraculous those seven years, enjoying amazing fellowship with God just fine, and I wasn't asking or looking for any dramatic or new understanding. In this vision I could hear the specific sins of America mocking God, "You are not God! If You are God, do something!" To me, the sound was maddening. The best way for me to describe it would be to share Isaiah 6:5, "And I said: 'Woe is me! For I am lost; for I am a man of unclean lips, and I dwell in the midst of a people of unclean lips; for my eyes have seen the King, the LORD of hosts!'" I can't claim that I saw the King; He was cloaked from my sight (to preserve my life, I believe). Just being in His proximity, however, produced these unspeakable understandings of the vileness of sin, His cleanliness and how the two don't mix, at all.

Furthermore, I shared in being held accountable for the sins of America. What? I cried out to God, "Haven't we been working wonders together? Don't You remember giving me that truck for my birthday?" But the overwhelming burden I felt left no room for argument. I, the Church, was unquestionably accountable for the horrible sounds echoing through God's Holy domain. With my face on the floor and my hands covering my ears from the maddening sounds, I exclaimed, "I'm sorry, Lord! I'm sorry, Lord! I'm sorry, Lord!"

For days afterward, I plead with God for the grace to tell

people everywhere about the atoning blood of Jesus Christ, the Lamb of God that took away the sins of the world, "Surely, they will listen, Lord, if You inspire them. Let me tell them that their sins are forgiven; surely they will turn away from continuing in them." It was a month later when I woke and heard the call to Michigan, where the building with its land was eventually given to me outright.

God does not force His will on anyone. I agonize when others are not ready to accept this intimate, personal relationship with God. In North Dakota I quit ministering a million times, in my prayer closet. Just as many times on the way home from delivering sermons, "I quit! I quit! I quit, God!" He often responded, "I *like* your voice, Robert. *I want* to hear you preach. *I'm* listening. You are ministering to *Me*, son. To see your faithfulness and hear you stand up for what I've told you blesses My heart to no end. You are part of the salt of the earth that gives me reason to keep America." He convinced me through these intimate expressions of affection that I wasn't wasting my time, making it worth it for me to live for Him.

During the times of my agonizing frustration, I was looking for air traffic control type results. "Turn now." And what did they do in ATC when I said that? They turned now! As an air traffic controller, my instructions were not an option to my listeners. I had control over them. In contrast, a minister might say, "That is leading to death and therefore not pleasing to God. Turn. Choose life!" And instead of seeing a turn take place, the minister will hear 1,000 reasons from the sickly, self-sufficient person why their behavior is okay. In both cases I can see death and disaster coming! Back then

I was in control and the flights were somewhat like puppets, to their benefit. Now, only God is in control. When instructions or insights are given, they are left to the listener's free will. God honors the choice of man and refuses to violate this super precious gift. This built-in friction of ministry grinded on me, to say the least. In truth, it has become the inmost agony of my life, even greater than my own 9/11-style collapse, when I resisted God until I hit the absolute bottom. He graciously picked me up from there, and it is my prayer to help others avoid disasters and falling as deep and hard as I did, or falling at all.

This is where I have learned to share in Jesus' suffering now. Yes, He suffers today. To offer someone the most valuable and life-saving and life-changing things they could ever hope for, even things they have probably specifically prayed for, to offer them a God-secured blessed future of their own and then see them consistently reject those things for what is a pile of poop in comparison–well, it is excruciating. So, for years, I see people languish. I pray. I intercede. I wail in reverent submission to God. Some break through. Many do not, but deteriorate instead. This has brought me into measures of Jesus' suffering that I did not previously understand existed. I do believe it's called, simply, patience. Older versions of the Bible call it long-suffering and I'm thinking that's a good translation. It turns out that sharing in Jesus' suffering is a necessary way for any child of God to share in Jesus' inheritance. (Romans 8:17)

When I issued commands as an air traffic controller, occasionally I would have to order a correction that didn't sit well with the pilot, especially if the pilot brought on the hazard himself. But there is a place in intimacy with God in which no matter what He says, it tastes as sweet as honey, even unpleasant words of woe, because their objective is to help mankind. Oh, how my heart longs for everyone to know that very *wise* place!

While serving in Michigan, ND, we have also been dispatched to minister in various churches within this state, across America, and overseas. I had been invited to minister at a church in Texas. In the weeks leading up to my scheduled time to speak there, God revealed to me that the people where I was going had been mocking Him in the area of their finances. This was not something I wanted to go and preach about. These were God-fearing Texans, for heaven's sake. I'd much rather tell everyone about the unfathomable and indescribable riches of His grace, but this was a time to be firm, as one forged in the fire. As the date to speak grew closer, everywhere I turned I saw God's coming judgment. A pronounced picture developed that the lost and poor were not being saved from their misery because ministers of the Gospel were not being supplied with what was necessary to do their tasks. And indeed the pastors were being robbed of what was their personal portion as a ploy of the enemy to hinder the progress of the Gospel. God takes that very seriously.

When the date finally came to minister, I stood on stage being introduced by the Senior Pastor with God's message burning within me. I intended to give the people a ration, just as I so boldly told those who survived Hurricane Katrina of their need to repent.

After the pastor introduced me and passed me the mic, I

started, "I don't care if it takes a lightning bolt to strike right here, right now to accomplish God's will! I'm not only okay with that, I'm like, 'Please God, bring it!' Let me share just a little bit of scripture with you from Psalm 29." I began reading at verse three.

"The Voice of the LORD is over the waters. The God of glory thunders, *right now*!" I exclaimed. As surely as the Lord lives, when the words "right now" crossed my lips, a violent, building-shaking bolt of lightning struck immediately overhead. Everyone in the building heard and felt this profound, body penetrating wallop of thunder that was so obviously right where we were.

I went on with the sermon, void of any other evident lightning or thunder nearby, and gave them the ration I was sent to deliver. There was massive repentance. Some folks got out of their seats and went to wail, crying out to God, facing the walls. Others got to the floor, repenting before God. The church went from being deep in the red financially that day to having an abundance of finances. That day things were made right. That was God's grace pushing back, giving people the opportunity to repent.

But not everyone did. Within three days of that message being delivered, stories came in regarding unusual hardships that had overcome some who were present. Listen, I've seen too many "coincidences" to doubt God's blessings of comfort as well as blessings of scourge. It's an honor to be disciplined by God. He does it now, so that we can avoid days of adversity in the future, because He loves us and wants what is best for us. I hope my heart comes across properly to relay that God's anger was directed at improper actions, not the people. These were some of the sweetest and seemingly most loving people I had ever met. God corrects those He loves, those He delights in. It's all too easy to point our fingers at the people in that church, but I'm quite sure God could enter any congregation in America and find people who need to be disciplined. We don't naturally see things the way He does and we all need His point of view more than anything else. There's no such thing as love without correction.

Do I go and beat people down with insights like that? No! I wrestle with God, interceding for the good of humanity, as He expects of me, until He gives me a word of hope and healing to share, which, yes, sometimes does include issuing warnings. That's real work.

And now, just as we were given revelation ahead of time about moving away from Florida, we have hit a gusher of revelation that has shown us that God is calling us out of North Dakota, to something. God is calling us to something new, as we continue our journey of sharing God's message to the Church across America and beyond. Where this new season of journey will lead us is yet to be seen. Just like at other times in our surrender to Jesus, our future is a blank slate right now, given to Him and we walk like little, love-dependent children before Father God.

Our plan is to wait at the feet of Jesus, praying and watching, just the way I used to sit in tranquility in the East Coast waters of Florida, waiting and watching for my heaven on earth to come rolling toward me, perfect waves to catch and become one with. God has revealed that our incoming waves of grace will include visiting churches to minister, and that

He will also use us to bless other pastors' lives as answers to their very own prayers, to help them fulfill their calling. When I think of the two pastors who lent me their microphones, the ones I told you about within these pages, and how God used me to bless their endeavors, it gets me all fired up and ready to "Go!" I pray and watch for the divine waves, so excited for their coming, as we also aspire to be faithful with the day-to-day ministry tasks before us. His waves of love, grace and power will continue to pick us up and carry us along as we are being sent by God to make a Christ-centered environment wherever we go.

No doubt, we feel like parents who have given birth, through the most difficult of labors, to the church in Michigan City, ND. It is God's baby and that entitles it to all sorts of unstoppable heavenly privileges. God grew genuine love in our relationships with the few people who have regularly attended our worship gatherings. We have a true and selfless desire to see them benefit through every part of their lives. Something has begun here that can't be stopped. I expect to clearly see all of the ripple effects when I enter into the fullness of the presence of the Lord after I leave the earth permanently. God deserves the glory for what we have done in North Dakota, because we can most sincerely share that we could not have done it without Him. We have full confidence He will watch over it, water it, protect it, and we look forward to visiting it over the coming years to see what He's done with it.

Our friends in Michigan City have chosen, under Christ's personal direction to them, to make me their overseer. Check Paul's words in Colossians 2:5, "For though I am absent from you in body, I am present with you in spirit and delight to see how orderly you are and how firm your faith in Christ is."(NIV) He governed from afar, physically, but supernaturally knew things only Jesus could know through his personal relationship with Him. In Anglican terms, that would make me a bishop. I prefer being called brother, pastor, or overseer rather than bishop, since I'm only overseeing one congregation right now. Also the term overseer fits because of the prophetic gifting from God that I have shared with you through these pages. For God's glory and purpose, I humbly submit to this position and calling.

God is the Author and Finisher of our faith. And we've found He is serious about getting His reality into our earth. He wants to put His weight (merciful glory) upon our world. After forsaking all to be with Him, everything on earth pales in comparison, to say the least. Proper stewardship of all earthly wealth then becomes much more practical, efficient, and profitable for God's existing and ever-expanding Kingdom. This is what seeking His righteousness and placing His kingdom first looks like.

We are helping to build orphanages in Africa and India, too, via prayer, financial support, and physical visits. We believe God has entrusted these two orphanages to us, ones that have fallen between the cracks, you might say, of large organizations. Also, I have ordained three different men in service to Christ's Church, two at the local assembly in Michigan City and one stemming from my visitations to prisons in Florida. These things are a very real part of our journey, but till now, we haven't given a lot of thought to telling others about them. They have just been quiet parts of who we are, things that our Lord issues, esteems, upholds and protects. I share them with you now as a shining city on a hill, to demonstrate God's expansion of His Kingdom on earth.

I leave you with rock solid counsel regarding walking in God's will for your life, to actively build for yourself an unshakable, God-secured future, so that you do not have to suffer what I did through 9/11. God stretches us to look beyond and think beyond the ordinary. He wants to solve our natural problems through having us choose to respond to them supernaturally–not by conventional means, but through spending time with Him in His Word to see things from His point of view and living out our lives from there, in any and every given situation.

God came to the same surfing, ATC-adrenaline junkie, go-and-conquer-the-challenge creature He had good intentions for. I truly feel as though I have been built for this thrilling life with Him. Now I know, I mean really *know* in my heart, that He is with me and will never leave me, and that adversity, like 9/11, can strengthen me so that, among other things, I can better help others. In the face of impossibilities, faith in Jesus feeds me and His exuberant, exhilarating life rises from within me. Fully alive and fulfilled, all of my heart exclaims, "God is going to be glorified!"

A SINNER'S PRAYER

It's the attitude of your heart that counts, and whatever words overflow from there. If you believe in your heart that Jesus paid the price for your sins by dying in your place for them, and that God raised Jesus from the dead–making Him Lord of all–and that belief overflows from your heart and out of your mouth, then you will be saved. That's a paraphrase of Romans 10:8-13, and the assurance of salvation is based on God's faithfulness to Himself (His Word).

The following suggested prayer is not a magic formula, but it can help you voice the sentiment of a heart that is ready to be saved.

"Jesus, I have sinned. Thank You for taking away all of my sins through Your work on the Cross, making me fit for Father-God's presence, approval, and blessing. I accept You as my only Savior and choose to make You my only Lord. Help me with these choices every day, and help me to know and love God more and more. I give You control of my whole life, and invite You to make me the person You want me to be. Thank You for hearing my prayer and answering with miracles."

Mind you, there's no way to be saved without becoming God's possession. If this suggested prayer is the sentiment of your heart, you are voicing that you are offering your life to Him in response to what He has done for you. If your heartfelt, spoken offering is authentic, it will invoke His presence and cleansing, manifesting what took place at the Cross, and He will be with you, treasuring you forever. Go to Him in His Word and through prayer every day. He will credit you with amazing things and teach you to follow Him wholeheartedly.

ABOUT THE AUTHOR

Formerly an air traffic controller, author Robert S. Totman and his wife Susan are missionaries with four children. They are gifted speakers who consider invitations to anywhere, pioneers who have planted a community church in North Dakota, and founders of Bethesda Global Ministries. Visit Robert S. Totman on the internet at www.RSTvictory.com or email him directly at Robert@RSTvictory.com.

"And they will say, 'This land that was desolate has become like the garden of Eden, and the waste and desolate and ruined cities are now fortified and inhabited.' Then the nations that are left all around you shall know that I am the LORD; I have rebuilt the ruined places and replanted that which was desolate. I am the LORD; I have spoken, and I will do it."
Ezekiel 36: 35-36 (ESV)